So These are my 50's... Really!?!

How to Laugh, Live and Love Yourself Throughout the Decade

Coralee Caldwell

Contents

Introduction

Are you staring down the barrel of your 50th birthday with equal parts of excitement and trepidation? Or, perhaps you are already in your 50s? Well, strap yourself in, because this decade is a wild ride, filled with unexpected twists and turns, and a whole truckload of laughter... trust me, you will need it.

This is not your average, dry self-help manual. It's a sassy, women and science-based guide to navigating the challenges, the joys, and the downright weirdness of your 50s. For those reading this in print, I solemnly promise to always use a size 12 or larger font in this book! Otherwise, we'll all be searching for our newly acquired 1.5 readers! For those of you reading on Kindle, now is the perfect time to size up!

Buckle Up, Buttercups: It's Time to Rock Your 50s

Turning 50 is a milestone that echoes with excitement and fear for many women. It is a whispered promise of change, and possibly a turning point. However, the media's narrative of turning 50 often clouds our judgment, painting a picture of wilting flowers, fading dreams, and a slow decline into a state of irrelevance. Well, that's a load of crap.

Times have changed and beige cardigans, matching twinsets, and sensible shoes won't feature here. This book isn't your mother's, or grandmother's guide to aging gracefully. It is about embracing the magnificent reality of our 50s, even the wrinkles and saggy arms. It's about zipping up the loudmouthed societal BS and celebrating the badassery that comes with the benefits of being a woman. You might fit into the category of someone who has seen it all, and perhaps even done some things she shouldn't have, but hey, who is judging, that's life, and that's you!

I am a well-seasoned traveler on this journey of self-discovery, or whatever you wish to label it. I embrace laughter and sisterhood. I have some pretty hilarious stories to share about myself and hundreds of incredibly amazing women who are redefining what it means to be fabulous in their 50s. Think of Cyndi Lauper's words in her timeless song, "Girls Just Want to Have

Fun." This deeply resonates with women in their 50s who are redefining the essence of *fabulousness*. The song's empowering message of liberation strikes a chord with women, reflecting our desires to break away from societal pressures and embrace our true selves. In this stage of life, we find a renewed sense of confidence and liberation, valuing joy, fulfillment, and self-expression above conforming to societal standards. Just as the lyrics imply, we assert our right to enjoy life, be authentic, and chart our own paths, underscoring the fact that age should never hinder one's ability to live boldly and magnificently (Wikipedia, 2019).

This is a vibrant, complex journey and sometimes an utterly bewildering time. It doesn't matter if you are in your mid-50s, late 50s, or just about to be 50—this book will serve as a virtual confidante, a trusty guide, and a constant companion to dip into when you need to.

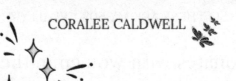
Why Read This Book?

Perhaps the image of our cover model, Kate, intrigued you, and you are eager to unravel the mystery of turning 50. Maybe you are seeking solace in some shared laughter amidst the chaos and confusion, or you've just found yourself knee-deep in the beauty of the absurdity of it all. Whatever your reason, you are here in good company. You are the protagonist of this narrative. Your hopes, fears, triumphs, and tribulations are all woven into the fabric of these pages. As we navigate the twists and turns of your 50s, remember this—you are not alone.

If you are looking for a wordsmith who has a penchant for wit, a dash of quirkiness, and a heart as big as the ocean—you have chosen the right author. I encapsulate the essence of a woman who has seen her fair share of life's ups and downs, yet still finds joy in simple pleasures from pasta, puppies, and people, to the occasional philosophical pondering. (An alliteration of P's—I didn't realize that till right now. How IRONIC that P's snuck up on me!!! This is a golden-glitter example of a 50-something moment!).

Here's a sneak peek of what awaits you:

- **Humor:** Get ready to laugh; be it a snicker, a snort, or a loud explosive reaction, you will enjoy reading your way through anecdotes and observations that'll have you nodding in recognition and rolling with laughter. You might need to cross your legs tightly (you know what I mean). From the hilarity and frustration of hot flashes to the ridiculousness of forgetting where you parked your car (again). These pages are packed with comedic gems that'll leave you in stitches.

- **Lightheartedness:** Say goodbye to stuffy, solemn tones, and hello to a breezy, conversational style that feels like chatting with an old friend over a cup of coffee, or glass of wine. As we navigate the highs and lows of your 50s, expect a touch of whimsy, a dash of sarcasm, and a whole lot of heart.

- **Knowledge with evidence:** Dive deep into the science behind the changes you're experiencing, with a sprinkle of research-backed insights to enlighten and empower you on your journey. From the hormonal rollercoaster of menopause to the cognitive changes that come with age, arm yourself with knowledge and emerge stronger, wiser, and ready to tackle whatever life throws your way.

- **Practical activities:** From actionable steps to thought-provoking exercises, each chapter offers practical tools to help you navigate the murky waters of your 50s with grace and gusto. Whether you're looking to revamp your skincare routine, reignite your passion for hobbies, or rediscover your sense of purpose, these pages are brimming with inspiration to help you live your best life.

- **Funny graphics:** Keep an eye out for quirky Kate icons and whimsical graphics sprinkled throughout the book, adding a dose of delight to your reading experience. These sassy illustrations, these visual treats are sure to bring a smile to your face as you journey through the pages of this book.

As you stand on the brink of this new chapter in your life, you may find yourself wondering what lies ahead. Having this book as a source of wisdom and laughter in your toolbox is a great asset as you navigate the wild ride of your fifth decade.

Each chapter is divided into four delightful subsections:

1. Let's Learn About It

Delve into the nitty-gritty of the subject at hand, blending research-based insights with juicy anecdotes and unmentionables that'll have you nodding in recognition.

Forget everything you think you know about turning 50. In these pages, we'll delve deep into the latest research, debunking myths and uncovering the "secret knowledge" they never taught you in health class. From the physiological changes to the emotional rollercoaster, we'll explore it all with a healthy dose of humor and relatable anecdotes.

Understand the science behind what's happening to our bodies and minds. From hot flashes to unexpected changes in our "downstairs neighbors,"

(aka Vintage Va-Jay-Jay, Golden Gateway, Mature Muff, Seasoned Snatch, Wisdom Womb, Senior Siren, Elderflower, Silver Slipper, Grandma's Grove, Vintage Vixen, Eternal Eden, or Granny's Grotto) we'll break the taboos and talk about the things no one else dares to mention. Because sharing the laughs (and sometimes the awkward moments) can be incredibly liberating.

2. Let's Laugh About It

Take a lighthearted journey through the absurdities and idiosyncrasies of life in your 50s, finding humor in the every day and laughter in the mundane. Life in your 50s is full of hilarious moments, and we're here to celebrate them all. From accidentally calling your boss "Mom" to wondering why your reading glasses are suddenly stapled to your forehead, we'll explore the lighter side of aging together.

Through embarrassing stories and shared laughs, we'll remind you that laughter is the best medicine, even when it's at your own expense, especially when you find yourself tripping over your own feet in the grocery store or forgetting what you were saying mid-sentence. We've all been there, and it's better to laugh along when enjoying life's blunders, big and small.

3. How to Engage With & Embrace The Changes

Embrace the change, because fighting it is a losing battle. Your 50s are a chance to redefine yourself, embrace new opportunities, and engage with the world in a way that feels authentic and empowering. Say goodbye to societal expectations and hello to reinvention, discovery, and maybe even a little salsa dancing (without pulling a hamstring).

Roll up your sleeves and dive into practical activities and evidence-based strategies to empower and embrace this new phase of life.

Engage with your amazing self as we explore practical tips, activities, and journaling prompts to help you thrive in your 50s. It's time to redefine beauty standards, reignite your passions, and build a supportive community of fabulous women who are ready to conquer the world.

4. Fall in Love With Yourself

Self-love can be tough at any age, but in your 50s, it's more important than ever. We'll explore ways to cultivate compassion for yourself, celebrate your unique qualities, and silence that inner critic once and for all because you're not too old for anything—especially not for falling in love with yourself.

Bask in the glow of self-love and acceptance, with evidence-based insights and heartwarming examples to help you embrace the unique beauty of this chapter in your life.

And finally, fall in love with the woman in the mirror. Rediscover your inner fire, celebrate your flaws, and learn to love yourself, wrinkles and all. Self-care isn't selfish—it's a necessity. So, let's nourish our bodies, minds, and souls together as we embrace this exciting new chapter of our lives.

This book isn't just for you; it's for every woman who's ever doubted herself, felt invisible, or wondered if her best years are behind her. It's a celebration of the power, the resilience, and the sheer joy of being a woman in her 50s. So, grab a glass of wine, put on your favorite comfy pants, and get ready for a journey of self-discovery, laughter, and sisterhood.

Because, quite frankly, our 50s are just the beginning.

Chapter 1
My Body

"If wrinkles must be written on our brows,
let them not be written upon the heart.
The spirit should never grow old."
– James A. Garfield

We will be taking a lighthearted approach to navigating the inevitable changes we go through as we "level up" in age. We'll explore a journey through the twists and turns of our ever-changing bodies, and how a healthy dose of humor can be your secret weapon in coping. We have been told countless times that aging is a natural process, but sometimes it hits us hard in the gut with the reality of all these changes. It is crucial during all these transformations to maintain a positive self-image, and ultimately, embrace aging with confidence. It's often our ability to laugh at ourselves that makes the journey even more enjoyable.

Let's Learn About It

"Wrinkles mean you laughed, gray hair means you care,
and scars mean you lived. "
–Unknown

Have you caught yourself recently doing a double take in the mirror? It's perfectly normal and a common occurrence. Or have you glanced at your peers, and thought, "Wow, she's looking older now," only to turn the gaze inward and receive a reality check of your own?

As that relentless clock of time marches on, our bodies travel on a fascinating transformational journey. How we deal with it depends on the timing and our mood. But here's the intriguing truth: These changes shouldn't instill fear, but rather present opportunities for self-discovery and acceptance.

Then there are the other changes that creep up upon us that no matter what, are going to happen. Let's take a look at some of these changes that come with aging (Swiner, 2021):

- **Brain health**: Contrary to popular belief, hitting the big 5-0 doesn't mean your brain is on a downhill slide. You may find yourself sharper than you were in your 20s! Realistically, there may be a slight dip in this "sharpness" around 55, but dwelling on it could make it far worse. Keep your mind in top form with a well-balanced diet, continue learning new things, play logic puzzles and word games, and keep up with what's current in the world. It's your brain—use it or lose it.

- **Menopause**: Oh, the joys of being a woman! Hot flashes, mood swings, dry skin, sleep issues, etc. And we thought periods were a pain in the whatsit! Fortunately, there are plenty of treatments and lifestyle changes that can help you weather the menopause storm. The best thing is, it does not last forever, I promise!

- **Mental health**: Remarkably, almost 95% of individuals over the age of 50 manage quite well through the tumultuous mood swings that accompany menopause, all without any additional cost, thanks to nature's gift.

- **Immune system**: Ah, yes one of the joys of aging—a much slower immune system and a higher chance of catching bugs from flu to Covid, RSV to pneumonia. Staying up to date with your vaccines, and regular health checks are essential as you get older. Again, a balanced healthy diet can work wonders to keep your immune system functioning well.

- **Hearing**: What's he saying? Can you repeat that? Huh? These are common phrases of a 50-something. Don't avoid a hearing test—being stubborn about it is not helpful to you or those around you. Get your ears checked out!

- **Bones**: Snap, crackle, pop! As we get older the sounds our bones can make can be compared to an old creaky floorboard in some ways. Weaker spots are more prone to cracks and splinters. Make sure your intake of calcium and vitamin D is sufficient, and get moving! Strength training exercises are good for you. Who knows, you may even find a new-found love for lifting weights and feeling athletic. Simply walking and keeping that body moving is so important to keep your bones healthy.

- **Muscle**: Loss of muscle is commonplace after 50 but good posture, regular exercise, and good food will keep your muscles in check. You don't need to aim to have Hulk-like strength (who wants to walk through doorways sideways anyway?). It could be yoga, Pilates, lifting weights, or whatever floats your boat to keep your muscles working.

- **Joints**: No, not that kind, ladies! Managing your weight and good hydration are the keys to keeping those joints well-lubricated and functioning. Osteoarthritis and other degenerative joint conditions are common and can become prevalent as we age if proper care and regular checkups are not done.

- **Heart**: As we get older, our heart needs a little more tender loving care. It is a muscle, and it also needs exercise to keep pumping well. A good diet, no smoking, giving your heart a little love, and letting it receive a little love, will go a long way.

- **Hair**: This could be called the silver lining of aging—literally! As the 50s approach, our hair may start to become thinner and turn gray. But going gray has become quite vogue! Even teens today are coloring their hair gray. Whatever you decide works for you, whether it is purple stripes, black, red, etc., it is what is on the inside that counts.

- **Skin**: Oh dear, those days in the sun without sunscreen are going to show now, or perhaps you were diligent and kept yourself slathered in SPF60. Age spots, wrinkles, and losing that elasticity are just part of the process. The best remedy is a big fat smile that will outshine any sun damage that may have been done. Another piece of advice is to schedule a check-up with a dermatologist if you have any concerns about moles or extreme sun damage.

- **Vision**: It's that time when we wish we had longer arms to be able to read the small print instead of acknowledging it's time to step up to reading glasses. Fortunately, these days there are so many awesome styles of glasses to choose from. Schedule eye tests regularly to keep on top of any changes in your vision that can be addressed earlier rather than later.

- **Health screenings**: Routine health checks start to become the norm. Keep in mind that even if you used to avoid doctors, early detection of any issues is critical. Rather be safe than sorry, because your health is important.

- **Unexpected health challenges**: Always listen to your body, stay vigilant about those tell-tale warning signs, and be proactive rather than reactive.

This list is not here to freak you out but rather to highlight some of the inevitable changes that are going to start happening as you age. Let's lighten things up a bit; keep reading as we have found some insightful and funny moments to share from various readers in an article in *Next Avenue* (Sapolin, 2013).

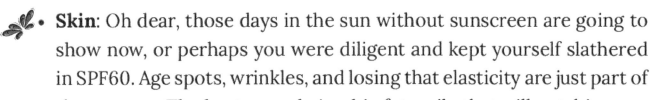

Let's start by delving into the science behind these transformations while avoiding excessive technical jargon and adding just the right touch of humor to keep it engaging.

There is some fascinating biology behind the wisdom—another word for wrinkles—etched on our faces, including the reasons behind those unexpected souvenirs of time, known as gray hairs, or in some cases the absence of hair where it once flourished.

Let's start with the gray hair! Ever wonder why our hair decides to embrace the silver fox look as we age? Some of you might just love this process and go with the flow of it, but others will continue with the relentless mission of coloring, highlighting, or whatever suits you to make you feel good about yourself. What is interesting, is the process of the "why" we go gray, whatever you decide to do.

Contrary to popular belief, hair doesn't magically "turn" gray overnight. As we get older, our hair follicles start producing less pigment, so when new hair grows it's more likely to rock the gray look, especially post 35 years old.

Scientists have been studying why hair turns gray, and they might have found an answer (Badshah, 2023). They think that stem cells, which can turn into different types of cells, might play a role. As hair gets older, these stem cells might get stuck and lose their ability to keep hair its original color. This study looked at these cells in mice, and also in humans. The researchers, led by a team from New York University, believe that if their findings are true for humans, it could lead to ways to stop or reverse gray hair. They found that these stem cells normally move around in hair follicles, which are like tiny pockets where hair grows. But as hair gets older, more of these cells get stuck in one place. The color of hair depends on these stem cells turning into mature cells that produce color. But when they get stuck, they can't do this properly, which may cause hair to turn gray. The researchers hope that by understanding how these cells work, they can find ways to keep them moving and prevent gray hair. While it's true that stress might make you shed more strands, the real culprit behind the graying phenomenon lies within our genes and the natural aging process.

Jo is a much-adored, elementary school music teacher in her 50s. Like everyone in her family, she has always been a very light blonde, so she didn't think it would make much difference when she decided to let her hair "go natural." One morning she was buoyantly navigating her cart of tone-chimes and Boomwhackers® through a kid-filled hallway, when she heard one of her 1st-graders say, "Oh, well I think she looks like a beautiful, old Grandma fairy!" Fortunately, she didn't run her cart directly into the brick wall ahead of her, and has since taken solace in knowing that this child was complimenting her! She chooses to focus on the "Beautiful Fairy" that she is!

In the end, whether you become a silver fox or not is mostly written in your DNA. Thanks, genetics! So, instead of stressing about the inevitable, maybe take a peek at your family tree for some hair color predictions. After all, whether you're leading a nation or just navigating everyday life, your hair's got its own story to tell!

Personally, I think gray hair is beautiful, but what you choose to do with your hair is an individual choice.

Now for those laughter lines and other skin issues!

Aging takes us all on a unique journey. For some, hitting the 50s is a huge milestone and means suddenly saying hello to neck wrinkles, forehead furrows, and those infamous "crow's feet," or what most prefer to call "laughter lines." Some breeze through this process without a wrinkle appearing until much later and they are the ones who can thank genetics and lifestyle choices that have shaped their aging process (Fischer, 2024).

The neck is a total giveaway to our age, long before the fine lines start to appear around the eyes and forehead. The neck is often a forgotten part of our body when it comes to skincare. Think of the times when you lathered on sunscreen over your face, having forgotten the poor old neck, leaving it exposed to harsh sun rays and weather. The skin on our necks is pretty darn thin, making it prone to wrinkling and sagging as the years march on. That smooth neck can suddenly be subjected to creases and folds that just suddenly appear!

 • Here's a fun fact: Your sleep position might be contributing to those neck wrinkles too. Ever heard of "pillow creases"? They're real, and they can lead to some serious wrinkling if you're not careful. Gravity doesn't do us any favors either, pulling down on our delicate neck skin and potentially giving us what's affectionately known as a "turkey wattle." Can you picture it?

There are many choices to make when it comes to our wrinkly issues: You could choose to do nothing, or you could choose surgery, or lotions and potions. Here are some tips for you to consider what best suits you to keep your skin glowing as you age (Davis, 2024):

1. Stub out that cigarette: Research shows that smoking can speed up skin aging, so kick the habit for a healthier complexion.

2. Say no to sunbathing: Avoid the sun's strongest rays between 10 a.m. and 2 p.m., and if you're outdoors, cover up with protective clothing and sunscreen to prevent freckles, age spots, and uneven skin tone.

3. Slather on sunscreen: Make SPF 30 or higher with both UVB and UVA protection your daily companion. Reapply every two hours for maximum defense against fine wrinkles and sun damage.

4. Keep an eye on your skin: Regularly check for signs of skin cancer, especially if you're fair-skinned or over 50, and see your doctor promptly if you notice any changes.

5. Moisturize, moisturize, moisturize: Combat dry skin by using a humidifier and hydrating soaps, creams, and lotions. If dryness persists, consult your doctor for further advice.

6. Nourish your body: A balanced diet and plenty of water can help repair and hydrate your skin from the inside out, so load up on nutritious foods and stay hydrated.

7. Explore anti-aging options: Over-the-counter creams and lotions, particularly those containing pentapeptides, can stimulate collagen production and give your skin a firmer appearance. For more intensive treatments, consider prescription options or professional procedures like Botox, chemical peels, wrinkle fillers, microdermabrasion, microneedling, or laser resurfacing.

8. Educate yourself: Know your skin treatment options, from injections to peels to laser therapies, and discuss them with your dermatologist to find the best fit for your skincare goals.

What They Didn't Tell Us

Remember those "birds and the bees" talks from your youth? Well, they might not have covered everything. I remember quite clearly waking up one morning and thinking "*Where the heck are my breasts?*" Much to my horror, I found them nestled in my armpits... moments like these, you just need to laugh about.

We'll share real-life anecdotes from women who have embraced these changes with grace and humor, demonstrating that laughter truly is the best medicine—even when it involves the occasional, and sometimes persistent rogue chin hair to the unexpected peculiarities and changes that accompany aging, including the fascinating and sometimes vexing effects of gravity on various parts of our bodies. Here are some snippets taken from an article titled: *The 9 Best Things About Being Over 50* (Sapolin, 2013):

1. **Aging with spirit**: Meriel Collins shares the valuable insight that age is not for the faint-hearted; it's for those with the spirit, the flexibility, and who still have an appetite for a quality life. So, as Meriel suggests, get that chin up and get ready to tackle each day with a big smile and a hefty dose of gratitude. After all, who needs Botox when you've got a positive attitude?

2. **Navigating college campus escapades at 70**: Sailing into the uncharted waters of our golden years sometimes finds us faced with a smorgasbord of adventures just waiting to be savored. Take Barbara Shramo, for instance, whose life brims with bustling college campus escapades as she approaches the ripe age of 70. Nothing slowed her down when she turned 50! She continues to expand her knowledge while working and keeps learning about whatever takes her fancy.

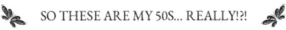
3. **Unstoppable adventure**: Ginnis Equality's boundless energy is truly inspiring, proving that age is a mere number when it comes to choosing adventure activities. From biking to kayaking to country skiing, she may not be the fastest but she is doing it!

4. **Reinvention and vibrant living in the city**: Pia Louise has some solid advice, in her reinvention of herself and a move to a city that thrives with vibrancy. She says, "Get up, keep goin'. You've come this far, be who you dream you want to be! Do it!" This is evident in her will to live, let loose, and have a ball after a reality check of not letting her self-esteem be destroyed by regrets of things she could not change.

5. **Rediscovering freedom in her 50s**: Syndee Leigh has found a whole new sense of freedom in her 50s that she hasn't felt since finishing high school. With grown-up children who are independent, she has gained a renewed sense of vitality and self-exploration without being bothered about what she looks like, slam-dunking societal expectations.

6. **Embracing life's laughter and new experiences**: The sheer joy and acceptance of laughing at herself and not feeling limited by the potential of possibilities is the elixir of life for Nancy Robinson who does things she may not have done before by saying "yes" to new experiences, and just going for it with the attitude of embracing the fun that getting older can be.

7. **Choosing freedom and new adventures**: Gaye Saucier Farris echoes this sentiment by relishing the freedom to now be able to choose what she does, and what suits her. Who says you can't teach an old dog new tricks?

8. **Inner growth and kindness personified**: The ability to understand what it means to focus on the inner self and at the same time share genuine benevolence with others when they most need it, has the reward of the deepest most positive effect on you, shares Sandy Interrante. Her positive energy is reflected in her life by just being kind, and purposeful in her behavior to others.

9. **Finding happiness in life**: Simplicity is sometimes the greatest gift to ultimate happiness. Choosing the things in life that give Jacqueline Burke a sense of well-being for herself reflects upon others positively. She gently shares, "I notice the beauty of nature more too. God is good. I can be as happy as I want to be."

Let's Laugh About It

The wacky world of being in your 50s is like stepping onto a rollercoaster where predictability takes a backseat to absolute unpredictability! It's a journey filled with moments that are both hilarious and sometimes hair-raising, leaving you with many riotous tales and stories that will make your tummy ache with laughter.

Life is undeniably more fun when you can laugh at yourself, especially in the face of the occasionally awkward situations that aging can throw your way.

Welcome to your personal laugh track, where we'll explore the comical side of navigating the world of yoga classes in your 50s, the ongoing quest for the perfect "shapewear" solution, and the uproarious mishaps that can unfold on the journey to fitness and healthy eating.

Let's start with yoga classes, shall we? Picture yourself, gracefully attempting downward dog, only to realize that your flexibility isn't quite what it used to be. Suddenly, you find yourself in a hilarious game of Twister, trying to untangle limbs and avoid toppling over—all while maintaining a serene facade. And don't even get me started on attempting to master the art of balancing poses; it's like a slapstick routine waiting to happen!

Now, onto the trials and tribulations of finding the ideal "shapewear." Ah, the lengths we go to for a smoother silhouette! From wrestling with Spanx like they're a formidable opponent to contorting yourself into what feels like a human sausage casing, the struggle is undeniably real. But hey, if laughter is the best medicine, then surely the absurdity of squeezing into compression garments is a close second!

And let's not forget the comedy of errors that often accompany the pursuit of fitness and healthy eating. Picture yourself enthusiastically whipping up a green smoothie, only to forget to put the lid on the blender (a real 50s "lapse of focus" thing)—a scene straight out of a paper towel commercial as spinach splatters all over the kitchen. Or perhaps you've had the pleasure of attempting a trendy new workout class, only to realize halfway through that you're in way over your head, flailing about like a fish out of water, huffing and puffing, while trying not to look stupid or collapse in a heap on the floor.

But amidst the laughter and the occasional embarrassment, there's a valuable lesson to be learned: A good laugh is just as transformative as a balanced diet and exercise routine. So, embrace the hilarity of aging, revel in the absurdity of life's little mishaps, and remember, and we will keep reiterating this, to laugh often—it's the secret ingredient to staying young at heart, no matter your age.

How to Engage and Embrace the Changes

This isn't all just about the giggles. Here we'll equip you with the tools you need to thrive in your 50s. We explore the playful side of aging, and embrace the unexpected quirks that come with reaching our "halfway point." Those laughter lines etched onto our faces are like badges of honor, telling stories of a life well-lived. Instead of fretting over these signs of the passing years, why not greet them with a smile and a sense of gratitude for the privilege of getting older—a privilege denied to many who don't reach old age? The realities of gravity's newfound influence and those unexpected moments of unwanted hair growth (because let's be honest, we've all been there!) or needing to suddenly cross your legs tightly are all part of sharing the fun and faux pas!

By embracing the humorous aspects of aging, we not only lighten our load of burdens but also challenge societal expectations, creating a more positive self-image. Rather than striving for unattainable standards of youthfulness, let's celebrate the unique character and charm that each passing year brings. Humor becomes a powerful tool in coping with change, allowing us to face shifts with resilience and wit. Embrace those hilariously awkward gym moments, to the comical miscalculations of our newfound flexibility;

laughter is a huge part of it all. It is not just a perk but a vital side effect that keeps us going. There's a silver lining in the absurdity of it all!

These topics that have been chosen for this chapter are those that are often discussed at length when hitting the 50s, signifying a pivotal juncture where changes to our bodies can take us by surprise:

Menopause

Ah, that mysterious time when your hormones are throwing a huge party and don't invite the rest of your body! There is no denying that this is a rollercoaster time of your life from hot flashes to mood swings but there is an end to it. That first hot flash takes many of us by surprise, as who wouldn't be when suddenly you feel this unbelievable heat building up in your body with nowhere to go and buckets of sweat start dripping off your body. It can be embarrassing, but yes, humor is a way to deal with it. I remember giving a eulogy at a dear friend's gathering, and suddenly a darn hot flash hit me! As sad as the moment was, I just had to ask someone to get me a tissue not only for the tears but for the sweat! I said, *Hey, I am in my 50s and I am hot!* I got a lovely round of applause that settled the awkward moment.

For those who are keen to try hormone replacement therapy, there are all sorts of options to consider (WebMD, 2023):

Pills:

Pros: Effectively relieves menopausal symptoms and reduces osteoporosis risk. Well-studied.

Cons: Potential risks include increased chances of strokes, blood clots, and side effects such as breast tenderness, vaginal discharge, headache, and nausea. Not suitable for individuals with liver issues or certain medication interactions.

Skin patches:

Pros: Convenient application and bypasses liver metabolism, making it safer for those with liver concerns.

Cons: May pose similar risks as oral estrogen, including mild side effects like breast tenderness, vaginal discharge, headache, and nausea. Skin irritation and sensitivity to heat and sunlight are potential issues.

Topical creams, gels, and sprays:

Pros: Safer for individuals with liver or cholesterol problems due to bypassing liver metabolism.

Cons: Less studied than other forms of estrogen therapy, potential for incomplete absorption, and risk of transferring estrogen to others through skin contact.

Vaginal suppositories, rings, and creams:

Pros: Effective for vaginal symptoms and may pose fewer systemic risks.

Cons: Limited efficacy for non-vaginal symptoms, potential risks of higher-dose formulations, and increased risk of endometrial cancer for those with a uterus!

When selecting the appropriate estrogen therapy, collaboration with a healthcare provider is crucial. Although oral estrogen is well-researched, newer delivery methods may offer distinct benefits and risks. Considering the uncertain long-term risks of hormone therapy, opting for the lowest effective dose for the shortest duration possible is advisable, with regular discussions with a healthcare provider to manage potential risks.

As for mood swings, well, getting those hormones under control will help but it is also just a time to accept that one minute you will be laughing, and then the next minute you may cry. It is different for everyone. If I feel myself becoming overwhelmed, I have learned to remove myself from the triggering moment and calm my thoughts with a few deep breaths. This is deeply personal and will depend on the individual and how they deal with it. But hormones being balanced will certainly help! And you don't have to explain to anyone why you want the bed covers on and then off, and then on and then off! Just do what makes you feel comfortable!

Embrace the Gray

I woke up one day and stared at my reflection in the mirror, a horrifying realization struck me! I was going gray! Panic overtook rational thought as the evidence was irrefutable. My once luscious locks were streaked with a gray invasion that was spreading like wildfire. I could have decided to be dramatic about it and shave my head! But then this didn't appeal to me, nor would it to many of us.

If you do decide to embrace the gray then you might consider a great short hairstyle, so that the multi-colored effect is not an issue to deal with. Otherwise, just let it be and let it grow out proudly showing the world that you truly embrace aging and the gray hair that comes with it. My theory was to proclaim myself as a wise wizard in training who loved my gray hair that came naturally! Over the years, the red carpet has seen countless fashion statements come and go. For decades, women have proudly embraced their natural beauty inspiring millions of fans. Icons, like Diane Keaton, Andie MacDowell, Merryl Streep, and Jodie Foster just to name a few, have made waves by showcasing their natural gray hair at prestigious events, flaunting their embrace of this natural process (Gelhoren et al., 2024).

Exercise Routines

Entering your 50s signifies a new phase in your fitness journey, where personalized exercise routines can unlock a realm of vitality and well-being. Rather than adhering to a one-size-fits-all approach, embrace activities tailored to your unique needs and preferences. Here's a rundown of exercise options crafted for individuals in their 50s, aimed at enhancing strength, flexibility, and overall health:

- **Strength training**: Engage in resistance training exercises to bolster muscle strength and bone density. Include squats, lunges, push-ups, and dumbbell curls in your regimen. Begin with lighter weights and gradually increase resistance as you progress. Aim for two to three sessions weekly.

- **Yoga and Pilates**: Embrace the mind-body connection with yoga and Pilates, both low-impact exercises that enhance flexibility, balance, and core strength. Attend classes or follow online tutorials focusing on poses that improve mobility and stability.

- **Swimming**: Immerse yourself in the invigorating waters of swimming, a joint-friendly activity offering a full-body workout. Whether completing laps in the pool or attending water aerobics classes, swimming fosters cardiovascular health, muscle toning, and stress relief on the joints.

- **Walking and hiking**: Lace up your sneakers and embark on brisk walks or venture into nature through hiking trails. Walking, a simple yet effective exercise, enhances cardiovascular fitness, strengthens bones, and uplifts mood. Gradually increase intensity and duration for optimal benefits.

- **Cycling**: Take to the streets or utilize a stationary bike for heart-pumping cycling sessions. This low-impact activity boosts cardiovascular health, enhances leg strength, and aids in weight management. Join group rides or spin classes for added motivation.

- **Tai Chi**: Embrace the graceful movements of Tai Chi, renowned for its fluid motions and meditative qualities. Tai Chi enhances balance, coordination, and mental focus, making it ideal for older adults pursuing holistic well-being.

- **Dance fitness**: Groove to the rhythm with dance fitness classes tailored for older adults. Whether indulging in ballroom dancing, Zumba, or line dancing, dancing offers a joyful avenue to improve cardiovascular fitness, coordination, and mood.

Remember to consult a healthcare professional before beginning any new exercise routine and listen to your body's signals to prevent injury. With so many activities at your disposal, maintaining an active lifestyle in your 50s can be both pleasurable and gratifying, laying the groundwork for a vibrant and fulfilling life ahead. And remember to ditch the one-size-fits-all approach and discover what suits you! While we are about ditching stuff, when it comes to shapewear, how about we get in shape instead! And if you are not into exercise who cares if you wear shapewear to smooth out those bumps that bother you, anyway?

Balanced Diet

As you enter your 50s, maintaining good nutrition becomes essential for promoting overall health and well-being. This pivotal stage of life often prompts changes in metabolism, nutrient absorption, and dietary needs, underscoring the importance of prioritizing nutrient-rich foods and balanced meals. Here's a closer examination of the key components of good nutrition in your 50s, accompanied by a selection of delicious and nutritious recipes to fuel your body. Place focus on nutrient density and opt for foods rich in vitamins, minerals, fiber, and antioxidants. Incorporate plenty of colorful fruits and vegetables, lean proteins, whole grains, and healthy fats into your diet.

Here are some examples of delicious and nutritious recipes perfect for those in their 50s:

1. Grilled salmon with quinoa and roasted vegetables

Marinate salmon fillets in lemon juice, olive oil, and herbs, then grill until cooked through. Serve alongside cooked quinoa and a medley of roasted vegetables such as bell peppers, zucchini, and cherry tomatoes.

2. Spinach and berry salad with grilled chicken

Combine fresh spinach, (my favorite is baby spinach) mixed berries, sliced almonds, and crumbled feta cheese. Top with grilled chicken breast and drizzle with a light balsamic vinaigrette for a refreshing and satisfying meal.

3. Lentil and vegetable soup

Simmer lentils with diced carrots, celery, onions, and garlic in vegetable broth until tender. Season with herbs and spices like thyme, rosemary, and cumin for a hearty and nutritious soup.

By integrating these nutrient-rich recipes and principles of good nutrition into your diet, you can promote your health and vitality throughout your 50s and beyond. Here are some other important facts to consider when it comes to nutrition.

- **Prioritize calcium and vitamin D**: With aging, bone health becomes of increasing importance. Ensure adequate intake of calcium and vitamin D to support bone strength and reduce the risk of osteoporosis. Include dairy products, leafy greens, fortified foods, and supplements as necessary.

- **Mind your protein intake**: Maintain optimal protein intake to support muscle mass, strength, and repair. Choose lean sources such as poultry, fish, beans, legumes, tofu, nuts, and seeds.

- **Stay hydrated**: Hydration is vital for overall health, digestion, and cognitive function. Aim to drink plenty of water throughout the day and include hydrating foods like fruits, vegetables, and herbal teas.

- **Watch your portions**: Pay attention to portion sizes to prevent overeating and weight gain. Practice mindful eating, relishing each bite, and stopping when satisfied rather than full.

Let's cast aside dusty stereotypes and outdated advice, and approach this thrilling chapter of life with enthusiasm. Life's too short not to laugh at the little foibles and surprises that make this journey uniquely ours. Remember that aging isn't a foe to be defeated—it's an exhilarating journey to be experienced with a newfound appreciation for our incredible bodies.

And, while we are at it, being healthy and eating right is of prime importance but so is having some fun, living your life, eating the cake, or drinking that glass of wine.

Engage, Embrace, Empower: YOU!

Chapter 1- My Body

ToDo 1- <u>Find</u> one new place where you can connect with others going through a similar time of life. Find a support group, book club, or workshop series at your local Y, craft store, library, coffee shop, etc. Once you do this, you will *feel* the intrinsic rewards, but as a reminder and an extrinsic reward, <u>buy</u> yourself one FUN barrette or hair accessory. Wear it as a reminder of the step you've just taken to improve your life!

ToDo 2- Get active 2x/week! Take a gentle stroll around the closest park or green space. If you have neither, or want to stay indoors, go to your local "supercenter" store and walk around the outer aisles 2-3 times.

ToDo 3-

Name a person or character who promotes a positive body image.	What do you admire, or inspires you, about them?	List 2 ways you could emulate what inspires you about them.

Falling in Love With Your Body

As you enter your 50s, you encounter a significant milestone in life, often accompanied by a shift in how you perceive your body. This period presents an opportunity to embrace self-acceptance actively and develop a profound love and appreciation for this incredible creation, your body, that has carried you through decades of experiences. Here are some strategies, drawing from science, psychology, sociology, and common sense, to assist you in falling in love with your body in your 50s:

- Practice gratitude: Take a moment each day to appreciate your body for all it does. Positive psychology research suggests that gratitude improves self-esteem and body image. Reflect on how your body supports you, allowing you to move and experience life's joys (Ackerman, 2017).

- Embrace aging: Understand that aging is natural, and each wrinkle and gray hair tells a story of a life well-lived. Embracing aging leads to greater satisfaction with appearance. Celebrate the experiences and wisdom that come with age.

- Nurture your body: Treat your body with kindness and care. Engage

in activities that promote physical health, like regular exercise, nutritious eating, and sufficient rest. Physical activity not only improves health but also boosts mood and body image perception.

- Challenge negative thoughts: Combat negative self-talk by challenging unrealistic beauty standards. Remember that media portrayals of beauty are often curated and unrealistic. Focus on qualities beyond physical appearance, like personality traits and accomplishments.

- Cultivate self-compassion: Be gentle with yourself and practice self-compassion. Acknowledge that everyone has insecurities, and it's okay to have days when you feel less confident. Self-compassion is associated with greater body appreciation and overall well-being.

- Surround yourself with positivity: Having supportive friends and family who uplift you and celebrate your unique qualities around you is so beneficial. Avoid comparing yourself to others, as comparison can fuel dissatisfaction. Focus on building meaningful connections and shared experiences.

- Seek professional support: If negative body image significantly impacts your well-being, consider seeking support from a therapist or counselor. Therapy can provide tools and strategies to challenge negative beliefs and develop a more positive relationship with your body.

Remember, falling in love with your present body is a journey, not a destination. It requires patience, self-reflection, and ongoing self-care. By incorporating these strategies into your daily life, you can cultivate greater appreciation and acceptance for your body at any age.

Chapter 1- My Body

ToDo 1- Your body is worthy of your love and praise! While we may not love every single thing, there is so much to be proud of. Stand in front of a big mirror and look at yourself through "ROSE-COLORED GLASSES." Find your eyes and say, "Those gorgeous brown eyes and lashes are my secret flirting weapon," or find your stretch marks and say, "Those marks show how I made our family grow," or find those forehead 11-lines and say, "These lines are there because I've had so many fun times and made happy memories." Go look in the mirror <u>now</u> and say out loud 3 authentic and positive statements about what you see!

ToDo 2- Take a LUXURY bath or shower. Get a new scrubby and your favorite scented soap or exfoliating scrub. Wrap your hair in a scarf for no-fuss afterward, add some bath bubbles or a fizzy shower bomb, have your phone play some 80's love songs, then sing out loud while you soak the night away!

ToDo 3- Schedule an appointment with your doctor or a holistic health practitioner to discuss where you are currently on the *peri to post-*menopausal scale. Confirm your feelings, ask your questions, and make sure you are taking the right vitamins, minerals, supplements, hormones, etc. After all, you can't love yourself if you feel lousy!

 # Fall In Love with: YOURSELF!

ToDo 4- Journal Entry: Reflect on three physical features <u>or</u> attributes that you appreciate about yourself right now, regardless of your society's standards or expectations. Write about why each of these aspects brings you joy or makes you feel confident in your own skin. Embrace the beauty and uniqueness of your body at this moment in your journey.

Ex: Features
Radiant, glowing, or soft skin
Graceful lines and wrinkles
Expressive, luminous, or sparkling eyes
Strong, shapely, or toned legs/ arms
Silky, soft, or healthy hair
Silvery or salt-and-pepper hair
Defined cheekbones or jawline
Soft, supple, full, or plump lips
well-manicured nails
Elegant, Strong, or multitasking hands
A confident, genuine, or warm smile
A womanly shape
Curves and contours
A tall and graceful posture
Toned, or healthy-looking body/muscles
Unique facial features

Fall In Love with: YOURSELF!

Ex: Attribute	
Poise, grace, and elegance	
Confidence and self-assuredness	
A confident stride/walk	
A sense of poise	
Commanding presence	
Inner beauty	
A personal, or sophisticated style	
Gracefulness movements	
Energy and vitality	
A warm, kind, gracious demeanor	
Inner strength and resilience	
A charismatic aura	
A radiance or glow	
Youthfulness and vibrancy	
A sense of comfort and ease	
friendly and approachable	
An aura of self-acceptance	

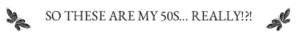

Fall In Love with: YOURSELF!

_____

_____

_____

_____

_____

_____

_____

_____

_____

_____

_____

_____

_____

_____

_____

_____

_____

_____

_____

_____

_____

_____

_____

_____

Fall In Love with: YOURSELF!

Fall In Love with: YOURSELF!

Chapter 2
My Romance

The best aspect of romance in your 50s lies in its transformation of a stage of your life where romance tends to take on a new dimension. This is powered by wisdom, experience, and a deeper understanding of both yourself and others. Significant changes in priorities, perspectives, and desires inevitably shape our romantic relationships during this phase. Stepping into your 50s finds many rethinking this whole thing about romance. It is a time when most of us are freed from the shackles of societal expectations (and many couldn't give a damn anyway, anymore!).

This is where we explore these evident changes observed in romance during your 50s, ranging from the redefinition of intimacy to the embracing of newfound passions. Our exploration will uncover the nuances and intricacies of love, companionship, and the connections you make in this remarkable stage of your life.

Let's Learn About It

Much will depend on your current relationship status, but there are always lessons to be learned when it comes to love, no matter your age. Let's just throw out the stereotypical script of what love is when you are 50 (what is that anyway?), and rewrite it with a good dollop of laughter, adventure, and if you drink, throw in a tequila sunrise or two!

Let's first debunk some common myths:

- **Myth 1**: *The dating pool dries up.* Well, no it doesn't, particularly the growing population of singles over 50 (Ritchie & Roser, 2019). Online dating platforms even have events and categories specifically aimed at this demographic. Go check!

- **Myth 2**: *Settle for less when you are older.* Never!! Being in your 50s often is a time when you are more financially secure, if you have taken care of your financial portfolios that is... but no matter what, the newfound self-assurance leads to a focus on quality connections over settling for an unfulfilling relationship or connection.

• **Myth 3**: *Romance is only for the young.* I have never heard such a load of crap! Love and intimacy are ageless desires. Sexual fulfillment and emotional connections can be just as vibrant as when you were younger, perhaps even better as mature couples bring experience and understanding to the table, (or the bed, or wherever tickles your fancy). There are many documentaries and films out there to show you that it's never too late for love, such as *First Comes Love* (HBO Documentary). Directed by Nina Davenport, this documentary follows the filmmaker's journey to explore the meaning of love and family as she decides to have a child on her own in her late 30s. Another is, *It's Never Too Late for Love* (Netflix). This documentary series showcases real-life stories of individuals finding love later in life, highlighting the unique challenges and joys of late-life romance.

What is ultimately the focus is to have the power to embrace the possibilities and define what a fulfilling relationship looks like to you. It may be a continued, long-term commitment/marriage, or maybe it's about casually exploring multiple new ones. The key lies in understanding your definition of what will bring you joy and pursuing it without societal constraints being imposed on you.

So, how do you do this?

• Reclaim your narrative. Don't let societal expectations dictate your happiness. Pursue hobbies, travel, and interests that ignite your passions. This not only enriches your life but also makes you more attractive to your current or potential partners who share your zest.

• Embrace online dating, though this is NOT recommended if you are already married! Platforms can offer a wider pool of potential connections who share your interests and values.

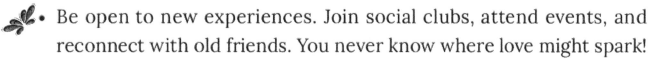

- Be open to new experiences. Join social clubs, attend events, and reconnect with old friends. You never know where love might spark!

- Remember, your 50s are a time of immense potential for love, connection, and personal growth. Don't be afraid to rewrite the script and embrace the exciting possibilities that lie ahead!

What They Didn't Tell Us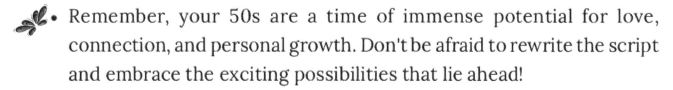

Entering your 50s can bring a whole new allure to love and relationships. It's a time that can also bring a blend of familiarity and excitement where couples have the chance to explore new dimensions in a secure and stable environment, which may have not been possible in their younger years. Whether you are facing the stage of experiencing empty nest syndrome, or perhaps you are one of the lucky ones who get to retire early—these two huge adjustments in our lives can come as quite a surprise.

They tend to bring along a bunch of dramatic changes that demand a fresh perspective, particularly in the realm of love and relationships. This is where the importance of fulfillment with whomever you choose to be with is key.

Physical activities, including sex, may pose another set of new challenges and delights. Changes to your body might impact your romantic life somewhat, but what is beneficial, is that the confidence gained at 50+ allows you to communicate your needs and desires.

The willingness to explore new avenues of pleasure can be refreshing for many in their 50s, and even take us by surprise! Intimacy and sex in your 50s will differ from your younger years so keep exploring new ways to keep that spark shining bright, be it through silly games and role-play scenarios. Simply prioritizing your quality time together is integral.

Actively exploring and navigating the evolving landscape of love and relationships is essential. It does change, and being aware of the importance of open and honest relationship communication about these shifting dynamics is crucial. Reflection on how your desires and priorities have evolved over the years, opens opportunities to nurture and strengthen your relationship, even if it was a good one before. You can deepen intimacy, strengthen your connection with your partner, and continue to evolve and grow stronger together.

If you are dating, then exploring the dating scene in your 50s can be both daunting and exhilarating. Don't shy away from challenges, and enjoy those comical aspects of modern dating.

Let's Laugh About It

Dating in your 50s should present lots of laughs. Share the funny stories and moments about online dating, blind dates, and those unexpected encounters, with your friends. Laugh, and laugh some more about those awkward moments and mishaps. Remember you are brave by putting yourself out there, and your date is more than likely just as anxious as you are!

Then there can also be the absolute epic failures set up by well-meaning friends thinking "*You two would be great together,*" which sometimes is not. Here's a little story to share about a friend who was set up with a blind date. Eager with anticipation, they arrive at the restaurant as they have been told that "*You would be great together*" thing. Anyway, they soon realize that they have absolutely zero in common. One loves to get out there on extreme adventures, while the other (my friend) prefers chilling with a good book or lounging at the pool. Instantly the conversation becomes awkward as they desperately seek somewhere they might have some common ground. Eventually, the absurdity of trying to make a situation work where it is not going to happen is clear, so they leave the evening as friends, each wishing the other good luck finding their "person." So sometimes even your friends don't know what you need!

For couples who have been together a while, things can get stale, and sometimes life does need some spicing up! A couple I know in their mid-50s decided it was time to attempt a dance class as they had never managed to dance well together, each thinking it was the other one who lacked rhythm. They were set and ready to go to class, bursting with enthusiasm, ready to impress each other and the teacher. However, it was not too long after the music started that it became evident neither had any rhythm. They stumbled over each other's feet, creating chaos and laughter in the class, soon putting that activity to bed. Despite their lack of skills when it came to dancing, what was clear was that they had the time of their lives in dance class. They streamed with tears of laughter at the hilarity of it all, creating yet another unforgettable memory together.

To close this section, here is one more hysterical story. A couple married for 32 years decided to spice it up in the bedroom. They discussed the scene, explored each other's fantasies, and came up with their sex adventure escapade. The mood was set with wine, candles, soft lighting, and good music. Blindfolds came out and then came the acrobatic position they had always wanted to try out. Well, tangled limbs, accidental bumps in the wrong places, the balance was lost, candles knocked over, and a curtain caught alight! Ripping off blindfolds, and hobbling from the unintended injury to grab the fire extinguisher resulted in slipping on the floor and giving the wife a black eye with the extinguisher! Well, the fire was put out and there was minimal damage but this story still brought them tears of laughter. Especially recently after the event when trying to explain the black eye...

In our 50s, laughter is what keeps us going, particularly in relationships. In finding the humor in situations, our bonds are strengthened as we create unforgettable memories together.

How to Engage and Embrace the Changes

Your 50s mark a vibrant chapter in your love life. While changes are inevitable, they can also be opportunities for growth and deeper connection. Here's how to navigate these shifts and embrace the beauty of mature love.

- **Communication is key**: Open and honest communication is the bedrock of any strong relationship. As priorities and desires evolve in your 50s, being able to express your needs and listen attentively to your partner becomes even more crucial.

- **Schedule regular check-ins**: Dedicate time each week or month to discuss your feelings, aspirations, and any concerns you might have about your relationship.

- **Practice active listening**: Pay close attention to what your partner is saying, both verbally and nonverbally. Avoid interrupting, and try to understand their perspective before expressing your own. Use "I" statements: Phrasing your feelings with "I" statements can help avoid defensiveness and foster a more productive conversation. For example, instead of saying "You never want to try anything new," consider saying "I feel like I'd enjoy exploring new activities together."

- **Embrace vulnerability**: Sharing your true feelings and desires with your partner can deepen intimacy and strengthen your bond. Vulnerability doesn't mean weakness; it's a sign of trust and emotional courage.

- **Express appreciation**: Let your partner know how much they mean to you. Tell them what you admire about them and express gratitude for their presence in your life.

- **Share your fears and anxieties**: Don't be afraid to open up about your insecurities or vulnerabilities within the relationship. Your partner likely shares similar concerns, and open communication can help alleviate anxieties together.

- **Seek support**: Couples therapy or counseling can be a valuable resource for navigating changes in your relationship. Therapists can provide tools for resolving conflict, improving communication, and rekindling intimacy.

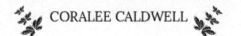

- **Reignite the spark**: Keeping the spark alive requires effort and creativity.

- **Explore shared hobbies**: Find new activities you can both enjoy, whether it's taking a cooking class, learning a new dance style, or joining a club together. Shared experiences create lasting memories and strengthen your connection.

- **Plan regular date nights**: Set aside dedicated time for each other, unplugged from technology. Plan unique date nights that cater to your current interests, be it a romantic dinner, attending a concert, or exploring a new part of town.

- **Travel together**: Planning a trip, whether a weekend getaway or a longer adventure, creates lasting memories and fosters a sense of shared experience and excitement.

Chapter 2- My Romance

ToDo1- Create a shared vision board w/partner or friend:
Participating in this activity together can deepen your connections with each other. The board displays images, words, and affirmations that visually represent your shared dreams and aspirations. It is a symbolic statement of resilience and a reminder of unity and purpose.

1. Gather magazines, images, quotes, and materials that represent both of your dreams and ambitions. Or, you can buy a Vision Board book that you both like. It is designed to make this process very simple.

2. Arrange these elements on a board or poster as a collage. Focus on themes or areas of your lives you wish to improve or transform.

3. Place your vision board in a prominent location where you'll both see it regularly, allowing it to inspire and remind you of your intentions.

4. Enjoy looking at what you created together!

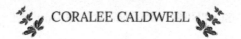

Engage, Embrace, Empower: YOU!

ToDo 2- Bucket list:

Everyone should have a bucket list at some stage of their lives, but creating one with someone you deeply care about adds special significance. Each item crossed off on the list celebrates your bond and the depth of your love for each other. Give it a try!

Our Adventurous Lives Bucket List	
1	16
2	17
3	18
4	19
5	20
6	21
7	22
8	23
9	24
10	25
11	26
12	27
13	28
14	29
15	30

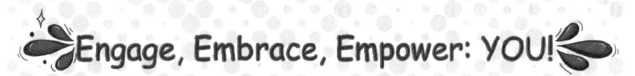

Engage, Embrace, Empower: YOU!

ToDo 3- Renewing of vows:

While not suitable for all relationships, renewing vows can be a poignant gesture, especially after overcoming challenges together that may have torn you apart. It serves as a celebration of enduring love and a reaffirmation of devotion to the journey ahead. You don't even have to worry about getting a license this time! Your vow ceremony can be as private or as public as you want it to be. There are no rules, but you CAN find lots of suggestions, information, ideas, and even scripts on the internet.

ToDo 4- Journal entry: Think about ways to reignite the spark in your relationship. How can you keep the excitement alive through shared experiences and adventures? Describe a recent activity or trip that brought renewed energy to your relationship.

Falling in Love With Your Love Life

Embracing your romantic status in your 50s involves celebrating the unique qualities that make you lovable. The beauty of mature love and long-term relationships offers a depth of understanding, trust, and shared experiences that simply can't be replicated in newer relationships. The whirlwind of youth settles, replaced by a quiet confidence and a deeper understanding of yourself.

Surround yourself with positive examples of love and happiness. Read stories about women who have found fulfilling relationships later in life or celebrate the strong marriages around you. Here are two inspiring stories to illustrate the depth of long-term relationships:

- Married for 62 years, this couple has seen each other at their best and worst, yet through it all, their love has only grown stronger. Admittedly while they may not have the same energy as in their youth, laughter, companionship, and a deep, true love have enhanced their lives together.

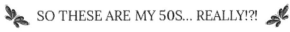

 After 45 years of marriage, this couple finds happiness in the small things. Simple but meaningful gestures like holding hands during a walk or sharing a knowing glance across the table without a word being spoken. There is no need for grand gestures and valuing the comfort of a shared silence together speaks volumes about their love.

Love stories differ, but what remains consistent is shared laughter, weathering storms together, respect, and a deep love that whispers rather than shouts, offering a sense of security and belonging that only comes with time.

The Liberating Power of Self-Acceptance

Self-acceptance and self-love are all about embracing who you are, wrinkles and all! When you feel good about yourself, it radiates outward and makes you more attractive to others. Taking care of your physical and mental well-being is crucial for a healthy relationship.

In your 50s, you've (hopefully) shed the insecurities of your youth. You've learned to appreciate the unique tapestry of your life experiences, the triumphs and stumbles, the scars and laugh lines. This self-acceptance is a powerful aphrodisiac, allowing you to step into relationships with confidence, authenticity, and a clear understanding of your needs and desires.

Consider the example of a young woman in her 20s who is constantly worried about being "good enough" for potential partners. In her 50s, with a successful career and a strong sense of self, she finally met someone who loved and respected her for who she truly was. "*Now, I don't need someone to complete me,*" she says. "*I'm already whole on my own. But having someone who appreciates that wholeness—that's priceless.*" (Source: Personal story).

Self-acceptance frees you from the burden of trying to fit into someone else's mold. You become a magnet for partners who appreciate you for your unique qualities, allowing for a more genuine and fulfilling connection. Healthy relationships are built on a foundation of self-love. Prioritizing your well-being, both physical and mental, radiates a confidence that attracts healthy partners. Self-care isn't selfish; it's essential for creating a love life that nourishes your soul.

Just think of that young 20-year-old, constantly putting aside her needs to please her partner. Exhausted and emotionally drained, she eventually ended the relationship. In her 50s, she focused on self-care, pursuing hobbies, nurturing friendships, and prioritizing her mental health. This newfound self-love blossomed into a newfound confidence, which eventually attracted someone who cherished and respected her boundaries.

Self-love doesn't mean neglecting your partner's needs. It simply means understanding that a healthy relationship thrives when both partners are whole and fulfilled individuals. By prioritizing your well-being, you create a space for a more balanced and fulfilling love life.

Embrace Your Status: Single, Dating, or Happily Married

Whether you're single, dating, or happily married, your 50s are a time to celebrate your romantic status. If single, relish the freedom and independence, exploring passions, traveling the world, and connecting with friends. Singleness isn't a waiting room for a relationship; it's an opportunity to discover the joys of self-sufficiency.

If you're dating, approach it with a sense of adventure. Don't be afraid to put yourself out there and embrace the excitement of meeting new people. Remember, dating is a process of exploration, not a desperate search for "the one."

For those who are happily married, cherish the connection built. Celebrate the shared memories, the quiet moments of understanding, and the unwavering love that binds you together.

Embracing the journey of traveling through the landscape of love after 50 is filled with possibilities. Instill open communication, rediscover shared interests, and embrace vulnerability, to create a fulfilling and vibrant love life in your 50s and beyond.

Fall In Love with: YOURSELF!

Chapter 2- My Romance

ToDo1- Date night challenge:

Plan a date night with your partner that involves trying out something new together. Take a moment to sit together and brainstorm ideas for the date. This could be a creative workshop, a new restaurant, skydiving, a cooking class, or practically anything you enjoy. Approach this date night with an open mind and a sense of adventure. Leave behind any distractions or worries you may have and focus on enjoying each other's company. After the date night, take some time out together to reflect on the experience with your partner where you can share thoughts, and favorite moments from that time together. Discuss how the activity brought you together and what it did to strengthen your bond with each other.

My Favorite Moments:

My Favorite Moments:

 # Fall In Love with: YOURSELF!

ToDo2- Love letter to yourself:

Set aside some quiet time and find comfortable space to grab a pen and paper, or your laptop, or however you prefer to write. Address the letter to yourself using your name or a nickname you may have. Pour your heart out, being honest, vulnerable and kind to yourself. Highlight the qualities and strengths you posses and what makes you lovable. Write about your proudest moments, your treasured memories and the things that make you so special. After finishing your love letter, take a moment to read it aloud to yourself. Reflect on how writing this letter made you feel and the insights you have gained from writing it.

Dear ME,

_____

_____

_____

_____

_____

_____

_____

_____

_____

All my BEST love, ME

Fall In Love with: YOURSELF!

ToDo3- Connection journal

This space is to write down what you appreciate about your special connection with a partner, friend, work colleague, etc. Think about meaningful moments you have shared. Write freely, with an open heart, allowing thoughts and feelings to flow without judgment onto the page. Consider how this relationship has evolved over time & find some words to describe what/how this connection makes you feel about yourself.

_____

_____

_____

_____

_____

_____

_____

_____

_____

_____

_____

_____

_____

_____

_____

_____

_____

_____

_____

 # Fall In Love with: YOURSELF!

ToDo 3- continued...

I feel accepted
I feel understood
I feel cherished
I feel valued
I feel supported
I feel empowered
I feel inspired
I feel validated
I feel connected
I feel fulfilled
I feel appreciated
I feel uplifted
I feel confident
I feel secure
I feel loved
I feel respected
I feel encouraged
I feel enriched

Fall In Love with: YOURSELF!

Chapter 3
My Mental Motivation

Self-discovery and empowerment are words that resonate deeply with the experience of being in your 50s. This decade of life is a pivotal time that encourages introspection, reflection and sometimes even the occasional incredulous thoughts, often punctuated with a big question mark.

It's time to go build an eco-colony and live off the grid, right? It's a period where the mind becomes the epicenter of change, guiding us through a transformative journey brimming with opportunities for personal growth and fulfillment.

Stepping into your 50s feels like the ground beneath you undergoes a profound shift, metaphorically speaking, of course. You may find yourself contemplating the choices you have made that have shaped your life's path thus far, reassessing your priorities, and seeking a deeper sense of understanding of your purpose in life. Mental motivation embodies resilience, enthusiasm, and the power of maintaining a positive mindset. The significance of cultivating such a mindset cannot be emphasized enough.

Simultaneously, it involves focusing on self-motivation and embracing a mentality of growth and possibility. Given the diverse experiences people have in their 50s, there is a need for insight, strategies, and inspiration to help you harness the boundless potential of your mind.

After all, these are your thoughts going through your mind, and it's time to make those that mean something to you reality, and not just cast them aside merely because it may not be deemed the *right thing...*

Let's Learn About It

Here are a couple of pointers to guide us through this internal exploration, offering insights into the mental and emotional dynamics that accompany this transformative phase.

• **Self-discovery**: Contemplating life's choices and priorities.

Entering our 50s feels for many like it's embarking on a profound voyage into the innermost recesses of our being. This juncture urges us to examine the decisions we've made thus far, contemplating their influence on the course of our lives. These moments of self-reflection frequently spark a reevaluation of priorities, urging us to realign our actions with our core values and long-held aspirations. According to Erikson's theory of psychosocial development, those in their 50s confront the stage of generativity versus stagnation, where the goal is to leave a lasting legacy and find meaning in their lives (Mcleod, 2018). This quest for meaning can propel us to delve deeper into our purpose, including grappling with existential questions that have long lingered in the recesses of our minds.

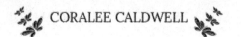

• **Empowerment**: Cultivating resilience and a positive mindset.

At the heart of the journey of self-discovery when reaching our 50s lies the cultivation of resilience and a positive mindset. This period demands unwavering resilience in the face of life's challenges, as we weave through the complexities of aging, relationships, and societal expectations. Resilience, defined as the ability to bounce back from adversity, serves as a cornerstone of mental motivation, enabling us to weather the storms of life with grace and fortitude (Southwick et al., 2014). Additionally, a positive mindset boosts empowerment, giving us the confidence and optimism to embrace change and seize opportunities. Studies have demonstrated that maintaining a positive outlook can enhance psychological well-being, reduce stress levels, and promote overall resilience (Boehm & Kubzansky, 2012). Thus, nurturing a positive mindset becomes imperative in gaining a sense of empowerment in our 50s.

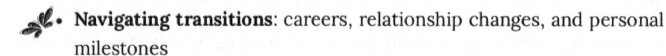• **Navigating transitions**: careers, relationship changes, and personal milestones

As with other decades, there are transitions to deal but when reaching our 50s, which is a little further than halfway for most of us, we are confronted with a plethora of life transitions, ranging from career changes to shifts in personal relationships. It can also be a time for career reevaluation, where we think about our professional paths and explore new opportunities for growth and fulfillment, sometimes heading in directions we never even thought possible. Research by Carstensen et al. (2024) indicates that those in their 50s experience heightened awareness of time, prompting us to prioritize meaningful experiences and relationships over material pursuits. This newfound perspective often leads to career transitions aimed at aligning our work with our values and passions. As a result, many of us

find renewed motivation and fulfillment in pursuing careers that resonate more deeply with our life missions.

Similarly, relationships undergo significant transformations in our 50s, as does the process of navigating the complexities of marriage, parenthood, and empty nesting. The empty nest syndrome, in particular, prompts us to reassess our relationships and redefine our roles as partners and parents. Studies have highlighted the importance of maintaining strong social connections and support networks for psychological well-being and resilience in later life (Umberson et al., 2010). This reassessment can deepen and enrich our interactions with our partners, and it can invigorate social activities that strengthen our bonds with friends and community members. Thus, building healthy relationships becomes paramount in promoting emotional fulfillment and empowerment in our 50s.

Personal milestones such as health challenges, financial planning, and retirement decisions loom large on the horizon, prompting us to confront mortality and plan for the future. The pursuit of optimal health and well-being becomes a central focus as we strive to maintain physical vitality and emotional resilience when reaching our 50s and continue beyond. The research underscores the significance of lifestyle factors such as regular exercise, balanced nutrition, and stress management in promoting healthy aging and longevity (Booth et al., 2012).

Entering our fifties offers a chance for real self-discovery, empowerment, and growth. It's a time when we're asked to face our deepest thoughts, feelings, and dreams. By staying resilient, keeping a positive outlook, and committing to our personal growth, we unlock endless possibilities to tackle the ups and downs of this decade with grace, bravery, and purpose.

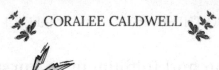

What They Didn't Tell Us

Society often paints the picture that our 50s are supposed to revolve around wisdom, fulfillment, and finally figuring out that your living room is for living, not just for show! Yet, here we are, many of us still trying to decipher the fine line between feeling wise and just feeling tired. Surprise, surprise, this era of our lives can also introduce us to feelings of being stuck, and perhaps suddenly grappling with anxiety and depression. It's as if we have been given free access to a horrible club we didn't choose to join! These feelings are very common, and it's time we started talking more about it. Being able to hear stories from women who have faced similar challenges, share some laughs and wisdom on navigating these times, and find ways to break free from feeling locked into circumstances can be immensely helpful. Exploring the benefits of mindfulness practices for mental health can include various therapeutic approaches, such as cognitive-behavioral therapy (CBT) which can be beneficial for addressing issues such as anxiety and depression (NHS, 2022).

The real deal with feeling stuck in your 50s

Now that you have reached the 50s you might find yourself feeling stuck in various aspects of life. This might manifest as pondering your life choices, career paths, strained relationships, or a lack of fulfillment in personal pursuits and wondering why you can't seem to move forward. Welcome to the fabulous club of the 50s where the only real requirement for entry is a sense of humor and the occasional feeling of existential dread...

Movies may sell us the midlife crisis narrative, complete with sports cars, crazy-long travel/vacations, and reckless decisions, but in reality, being in your 50s is more about finding your misplaced glasses (on your head), or

looking for your mobile phone (while on a call). Yes, it happens to others! The trick is to navigate this phase with resilience and purpose.

Here are some pointers to become "unstuck" and to provide some guidance to create a path that works for you. Think of it as your how-to guide to unsticking yourself.

1. To wriggle free from the midlife muck, let's talk about how to shift gears. It's like swapping out your high heels for comfy sneakers—still stylish but oh-so much more comfortable. Our values evolve, and suddenly personal achievements take a back seat to finding meaning, like finally understanding the appeal of bird watching or deciding to mentor someone who might think TikTok fame is a career path. Whatever it is that gives you some purpose, which could be pursuing a new hobby, volunteering for a charity, or engaging in an educational project, embracing this shifting of gears will lead to greater fulfillment of yourself.

2. Feeling a little nostalgic? Sure, you have perhaps had an incredible past with many experiences that have created who you are today, but things do change. In the past, we didn't have Wi-Fi! Now that is a great invention to embrace and use to your benefit. However, it is normal to sometimes get emotionally stuck in nostalgia and feel anxious about the future, especially considering the physical and emotional challenges that do happen to present themselves with aging can be overwhelming. Try not to put all your focus on what has changed, and practice that shifting of gears again to embrace the present with gratitude, cherishing relationships, and perhaps relish that silence that comes with the kids finally moving out! Don't worry, that will change as soon as the grandchildren start arriving! Cultivating gratitude for the present and appreciating the positives

can shift the focus away from the negative "stuff," and help create a sense of contentment and joy.

3. As for the relentless pursuit of personal success, it also has its change of direction which could be no longer about climbing that corporate ladder but perhaps instead building one for others to climb. Your wisdom is a treasure, even if it feels like family and friends might prefer to keep it buried at times! Your insight can be redirected with a focus on creating a positive impact on others. This shift reflects a broader transition from self-centered goals to a more altruistic outlook.

In essence, overcoming the feeling of being stuck when reaching your 50s involves a journey of self-discovery and redefinition. By embracing changing priorities, finding gratitude in the present, and aligning with a new sense of purpose, women can navigate this transformative phase with resilience and optimism. Rather than succumbing to stereotypes of a midlife crisis, they can emerge stronger and more fulfilled, ready to take on whatever lies ahead.

Breaking free from stagnation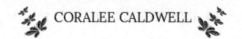

For many, breaking free from the rut and escaping stagnation isn't easy. Despite the challenges of feeling stuck in one's 50s, many women have found ways to break free from the cycle of stagnation and rediscover a sense of purpose and fulfillment. This could involve exploring new hobbies, traveling to new destinations, or pursuing further education or training. Feeling stuck is not exclusively reserved for this decade, so it is useful to have some plan if this happens later in life. The fundamental action is embracing change and moving forward instead of always looking back and wishing for change where change is no longer possible.

Sometimes marriages go through a topsy-turvy time during this period of change, and you might look at each other with sheer dismay or puzzlement. Who the heck am I married to? Did he always drive me nuts? Take a simple thing like the toilet roll and how it is put onto the holder, which now may become a huge thing, and you lose all sense of decorum when you find it the "wrong way." Finding this balance of what works to make you both satisfied, can make or break relationships if not dealt with. So, please continue to find the humor in the small things if you want to take your relationship to new heights. The 50s are fun if you make it fun.

Personal stories of women who have faced similar challenges and successfully navigated through them can provide inspiration and guidance. For example, a woman in her 50s who felt trapped in a monotonous job decided to pursue her passion for art and enrolled in painting classes. Through this creative outlet, she was able to rediscover her sense of identity and purpose, ultimately leading to a career change and newfound fulfillment. This, in turn, helped with her other personal relationships as she felt fulfilled and had a purpose.

Engaging with others who share similar experiences and aspirations is important. Support groups, community organizations, or online forums can provide a sense of belonging and encouragement, helping to feel less alone in this sometimes tumultuous journey.

The benefits of mindfulness practices

Mindfulness practices, such as meditation and yoga, have gained popularity in recent years for their numerous mental health benefits. These practices involve cultivating awareness of the present moment and accepting it without judgment, which can be particularly beneficial for individuals experiencing feelings of stress, anxiety, or depression. Mindfulness practice stems from Buddhism predominantly, but most religions have some form of meditative prayer or a technique that helps steer thoughts away from the usual thoughts that preoccupy the mind in our daily lives. It is not even about religion at all; it is about taking the time, even just for a moment, to quieten your mind and feel an appreciation for the greater perspective of life. These practices teach us to live in the moment, which is great news for anyone tired of trying to solve yesterday's sudoku. It also helps to reduce stress, improve mood, and enhance well-being—it's like a spa day for your brain without a hefty price tag! Research has shown that mindfulness-based interventions can help reduce symptoms of anxiety and depression (Hofmann & Gómez, 2019).

For women in their 50s, who may be facing unique challenges related to aging, caregiving, or career transitions, incorporating mindfulness practices into their daily routine can offer a valuable tool for managing stress, finding inner peace, and experiencing a profound transformation in life. From professionals finding solace in meditation to individuals discovering the joy of not thinking about work while doing yoga, mindfulness is showing up as the unexpected hero in many mid-life narratives. It's like finding an extra fry at the bottom of the bag—a small but significant victory rather than that feeling of expecting a last sip of coffee, and there is none left!

Here are some benefits of bringing mindfulness practice into your life:

1. Improving well-being enables the capacity to savor life's pleasures and cope better with adversity. Embracing the present diminishes worries about the future and enhances deeper connections, not only with yourself but also with others.

2. Alleviating stress helps to maintain a healthy heart and improve sleep quality. Integrating mindfulness into daily life can alleviate chronic pain and promote holistic wellness.

3. Mindfulness serves as a valuable tool in managing mental health issues such as depression, anxiety, and even substance abuse. Cultivating a sense of self-awareness and compassion can benefit emotional well-being and resilience.

Personal anecdotes of discovering mindfulness

Here are a few stories about different women who found that incorporating mindfulness practice into their daily lives helped them through introspection and self-discovery, making their journey of rediscovering their complexities and emerging selves easier and more courageous.

- A busy professional in her 50s struggled with chronic stress and anxiety related to her demanding job. After incorporating daily meditation sessions into her routine, she noticed a significant reduction in her stress levels and an increased sense of calm and clarity.

- Similarly, another woman in her 50s who was experiencing symptoms of depression found solace in practicing yoga regularly. Through mindful movement and breathwork, she was able to connect with her body and emotions more deeply, ultimately leading to a greater sense of self-awareness and emotional resilience.

- Lounging in the sand while on holiday and basking in the sun, a woman observed the scene around her—families busy with their children in particular, when suddenly a wave of realization hit her like a ton of bricks. She felt like an outsider, no longer fitting in with the family-centric narrative. She felt a profound sense of disconnection and irrelevance. Questions like: Who am I now? Where do I belong?

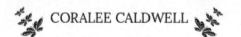

flooded her thoughts. Shifting her perspective of this panic, and being aware of the benefits of mindfulness, she then chose to make her holiday a journey of self-discovery, in pursuit of finding the way through the complexities of identity and purpose with her newfound, although puzzling at times, stage of life.

Exploring therapeutic approaches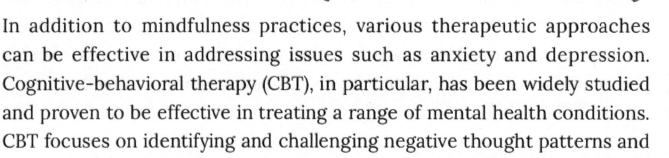

In addition to mindfulness practices, various therapeutic approaches can be effective in addressing issues such as anxiety and depression. Cognitive-behavioral therapy (CBT), in particular, has been widely studied and proven to be effective in treating a range of mental health conditions. CBT focuses on identifying and challenging negative thought patterns and behaviors that contribute to feelings of distress. By teaching individuals practical coping skills and strategies for managing stress, CBT empowers them to take control of their mental health and make positive changes in their lives.

Other therapeutic approaches, such as psychodynamic therapy, interpersonal therapy, and acceptance and commitment therapy (ACT), may also be beneficial depending on the person's specific needs and preferences. The key is to find a therapeutic approach that resonates with you, and that provides the support and guidance needed to overcome various challenges. While this array of therapeutic approaches may sound a little overwhelming, or a new alphabet to learn, each offers a unique path to understanding and overcoming the hurdles of mental health. Think of it as choosing between yoga, Pilates, or Tai Chi—it's all about what makes you feel centered, even if you are just there for the comfy mats! Experiencing the challenges of one's 50s requires resilience, self-reflection, and a willingness to explore new avenues for growth and self-discovery. Acknowledging and addressing common feelings of being stuck, or in a rut, exploring mindfulness practices

for mental health, and considering various therapeutic approaches, can enable women in their 50s to break free from stagnation and embrace this transformative period of life with courage and resilience.

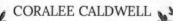
Let's Laugh About It

Sometimes finding the humor in a situation can be a daunting task. However, amidst the seriousness and introspection, there lies an opportunity to inject humor and levity into this phase of mental motivation, highlighting yet again the need for laughter and joy even in some darkness. Finding humor in the trials of the 50s is like realizing you accidentally started a trendy diet by simply forgetting lunch (the trend is fasting). Whether it's the comedic gold of attempting meditation only to compile your grocery list in your head, or the universal relatability of yoga poses gone wrong, laughter is consistently the secret ingredient to making this decade feel less like a crisis and more like an adventure.

Metaphorically speaking, it's like being stuck in the mud. There is even some humor in that when you try every which way to become unstuck but you just sink deeper—so how is that funny? Well, firstly it is quite funny seeing someone in reality stuck in the mud, because you would need to be a miserable person not to see any humor in that. Secondly, there is always someone to help drag you out of the mud, and if they fall in with you—that is even funnier. This brings to mind those two women whose video went

viral on social media. They were trying to empty an inflatable swimming pool by attempting to tip it over. Well, after much struggle, falling over, and countless times falling into the pool, they persevered and finally achieved success. They were also hysterical with laughter while doing this, engaging so many people who watched it to laugh along with them. The power of humor is immeasurable.

Another suggestion that is often given, and is given in this book too, is to calm your mind and meditate. This is not an easy thing for most of us to do. Empty your mind of all thoughts? It is virtually impossible. Whenever I meditate, I think of all sorts of things I haven't done, have done, want to do, shouldn't do, could do, can't do, etc. Never mind all the noise distractions from a peaceful bird tweeting in the distance to the darn neighbor deciding to mow his lawn when I wanted to meditate! It is hard work to shut it all out and there is nothing wrong with you if you can't. The point is to see the humor in it all and to have a little internal giggle or laugh out loud. It doesn't matter. What does matter is you are trying to quieten your thoughts and practice mindfulness.

This brings a thought to yoga which also has a good dollop of mindfulness when participating in this practice. It doesn't have to be solemn and silent unless you have joined a silent retreat (this could never work for me! Not speaking for days—never, not me!). So next time you catch your reflection in the mirror while doing the downward dog or any other contorted yoga position, it might not match the image you had in mind. Instead of being embarrassed about it—laugh out loud! I can guarantee you your fellow yogis will laugh along with you. If not, maybe find a better-humored class...

Another thing that many of us are ashamed of, is seeking therapy. Asking for help is a sign of strength not weakness, so get that thought straight! Starting therapy can be very intimidating, especially when you are in the waiting room patiently waiting your turn and not staring and wondering what your fellow patient's problems are. Be real, we all do it. This could happen—picture this...suddenly the door swings open, and you cannot believe it, but your therapist resembles a cartoon character! How are you meant to take this seriously? Instead of getting all worked up about it, see the humor in it, as the therapist surely does too. Once inside the therapy session, if you cannot find the power to just deal with it, the awkwardness will only intensify as you struggle to articulate your thoughts and feelings. Every word feels like a potential landmine, waiting to detonate into a cloud of embarrassment. Instead of dwelling on your discomfort, why not acknowledge the hilarity of human interaction and share a lighthearted joke with your therapist? After all, therapy is meant to be a safe space for vulnerability and self-expression, not a solemn tribunal of judgment.

Humor has a unique ability to lighten the burdens of mental and emotional challenges, offering a fresh perspective and a sense of levity amidst the seriousness of personal growth and self-discovery. By finding humor in moments of meditation, therapy, and mindfulness practices, we can transform our struggles into sources of laughter and joy. So the next time you find yourself stuck in the proverbial mud of life, remember to smile, laugh, and embrace the absurdity of the human experience. After all, life's too short to take it all too seriously.

How to Engage and Embrace the Changes

 • Take time for introspection: Reflect on your life choices and priorities, considering how they've shaped your journey so far.

• Embrace the present: Focus on the present moment with gratitude and appreciation instead of dwelling on the past or worrying about the future.

• Shift focus towards contribution: Engage in activities like volunteering or mentoring that align with your evolving values and aspirations for personal fulfillment.

• Find purpose in the present: Redefine your sense of purpose and seek meaning in everyday experiences.

• Practice mindfulness: Incorporate techniques like meditation or yoga into your daily routine to reduce stress and enhance emotional well-being.

- Embrace change: View life's challenges as opportunities for growth and transformation, seeking out experiences that inspire and uplift you.

- Maintain a positive mindset: Cultivate optimism and resilience by focusing on opportunities that arise from change rather than dwelling on setbacks.

- Prioritize laughter and joy: Find humor in life's ups and downs and surround yourself with people and activities that bring laughter and joy.

- Connect with others: Seek support from friends, family, or online communities who can offer guidance and understanding during times of change.

- Consider therapy or counseling: Reach out to a therapist or counselor for professional support in navigating life's transitions and addressing mental health concerns.

- Embrace vulnerability: Recognize that asking for help is a sign of strength, and be open to receiving support from others.

- Laugh at life's absurdities: Embrace humor in everyday experiences, whether it's the challenges of meditation or the awkwardness of therapy sessions.

- Cultivate a lighthearted attitude: Approach life with levity and playfulness, allowing yourself to laugh at imperfections and quirks.

- Share laughter with others: Connect with friends and loved ones through shared laughter, creating opportunities for joy and amusement.

By following these practical steps, you can navigate your 50s with grace, resilience, and a sense of humor. Embrace self-discovery and empowerment, and embrace the journey toward personal growth and fulfillment.

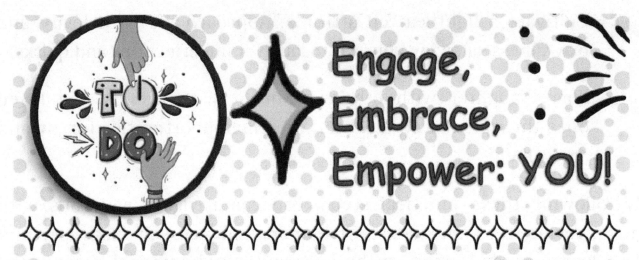

Chapter 3- My Mental Motivation

ToDo 1- Organize a Mindfullness-themed workshop (or girlfriends party), and enlist a professional host who experienced in leading small groups. This workshop should include guided sessions of meditation, discussions on the benefits of mindfulness practices for mental health, and interactive exercises aimed at promoting awareness of the present moment.

ToDo 2- Through sharing stories, a sense of empowerment and connection occurs. Topics like self-discovery, resilience, career transitions, and embracing changes can make fantastic stories. Try writing one of your own 50's stories (short or long), about a life experience you've had, then **post it** on a social media site, or send it out in an email group to friends. Don't underestimate the power and value of humor—incorporate it generously to create an uplifting and supportive atmosphere. You're writing this for yourself and for the benefit of your audience. Generate your story notes on the next page…

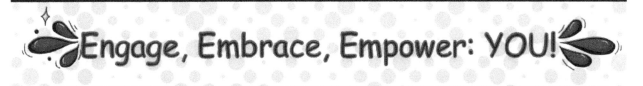

Engage, Embrace, Empower: YOU!

Start by telling who was involved, where you were, why, and introduce the main event/thing that happened...

What happened 1st...

2nd or next...

3rd, next or last...

Briefly tell how this experience changed you or your life. This is an easy place to drop in humor as you reflect on what you've learned and/oor how you've 'matured.'

Engage, Embrace, Empower: YOU!

ToDo 3- Jot down any reservations or hesitations you may have had about doing either of last ToDo activities. How can you address or overcome these challenges so that you can fully embrace the opportunities they would present to you.

Falling in Love With Your Mind

Ever tried falling in love with your emotions? Dr. Caroline Leaf, a renowned neuroscientist, mental health advocate, public speaker, and creator of the Neurocycle®, aka guru of all things brainy, spilled the beans in her podcast about why getting cozy with your feelings is the mental health equivalent of a bubble bath for your brain (Leaf, 2023). Dr. Leaf stressed the importance of embracing emotions rather than suppressing them, even if they are uncomfortable. She recommends that you don't hide from those emotions, even the yucky ones. Give them a big bear hug and say, I feel anxious/sad/excited... and that's okay!

According to Dr. Leaf, facing your emotions head-on is like giving your brain a deep cleanse, or detox. She emphasizes that emotions are like little messengers, tapping you on the shoulder and saying: It's time to do some soul-searching and grow a bit. So next time you feel your emotions are getting into a tangle, and trying to crash your party, invite them in for a cup of coffee and a chat. Take the time!

But wait, there's more! Dr. Leaf also emphasized that emotions should not run the show. They are more like traffic signals that are meant to grab your attention, not to take over the driver's seat. So, when you're feeling like you are stuck in a tornado of emotions, take a big deep breath, channel your inner traffic cop, and direct them into a safe place.

To help you become the master of your emotional universe, Dr. Leaf introduced her emotional signal guide. It is like a treasure map of your feelings, with four main types of signals: emotional, behavioral, physical, and perspective. So, grab your journal, jot down your emotions, and ask yourself some deep "why" questions. Who knows, you might just uncover the secrets of the universe—or at the very least, gain some insights into your emotional rollercoaster.

The importance of falling in love with your deep feelings and embracing all the emotions that sometimes may feel overwhelming at times is a means of improving mental health. So, go ahead, embrace those feelings, understand them, and show them who's boss! After all, a little self-love goes a long way in keeping your mind in tip-top shape (Leaf, 2023).

Amidst the chaos of life, we often forget to give our mental health the TLC it deserves. But just like you wouldn't skip leg day at the gym, you shouldn't skimp on self-care for your mind. Women who've unlocked the secret to inner peace and motivation through mindfulness, self-compassion, and positive vibes know it's not just a luxury—it's a lifeline.

Self-care isn't just about bubble baths and face masks (though those are great, too). It's about setting boundaries, prioritizing downtime, and doing things that light your soul on fire. So, whether it's indulging in a glass of prosecco, taking a walk in nature, or binge-watching your favorite show, make time for the things that make your heart sing.

Take, for example, a single mother juggling a demanding career, family responsibilities, and curveballs. Feeling overwhelmed and exhausted, she realized the importance of prioritizing self-care to maintain her well-being.

She began incorporating simple self-care practices into her daily routine, such as taking short breaks to enjoy a cup of tea, practicing deep breathing exercises to reduce stress, and setting aside time for activities she enjoyed, like reading or gardening. Through consistent self-care, this single mother found renewed energy and vitality, enabling her to show up fully for herself and her loved ones.

Finding inner peace through mindfulness practices is a powerful tool for cultivating self-awareness, compassion, and acceptance. It involves bringing our attention to the present moment with openness and curiosity, allowing us to observe our thoughts and emotions without judgment. Mindfulness is like a superpower for finding inner peace in a chaotic world. It's all about being present, tuning into your thoughts and feelings, and letting go of judgment. Whether it's through meditation, yoga, or simply taking a moment to breathe, mindfulness helps you find calm amidst the storm.

A mid-50s woman, who struggled with chronic anxiety and negative self-talk turned to mindfulness meditation to quiet her mind and cultivate self-compassion. Through regular meditation practice, she learned to observe her anxious thoughts without becoming entangled in them, allowing them to pass like clouds in the sky. She also practiced self-compassion by offering herself kindness and understanding in moments of distress. Over time, a profound shift was experienced in her mindset, which resulted in her finding greater ease and acceptance within herself.

The power of positive self-talk and self-affirmations profoundly impacts our mental and emotional well-being, not to mention our health! Positive self-talk involves speaking to ourselves with kindness and encouragement, fostering a healthy mindset and sense of self-worth.

Self-affirmations are powerful statements that affirm our values, strengths, and aspirations, reinforcing a positive self-image and empowering us to overcome challenges.

A woman in her late 50s struggled with feelings of insecurity and self-doubt when it came to her personal needs. She had no problem being affirmative in the workplace but fell short when it came to her personal needs. Through the practice of positive self-talk and self-affirmations, she began to challenge her negative beliefs and replace them with empowering statements. She repeated affirmations such as "I am worthy of love and respect," "I am capable of achieving my goals," and "I trust in my abilities." With each repetition, she felt a shift in her mindset, cultivating greater self-confidence and resilience. Positive self-talk became her daily mantra, with each affirmation guiding her toward a path of self-discovery and empowerment.

So, whether it's through mindfulness, self-compassion, or positive self-talk, remember to give your mind the love and attention it deserves. After all, a happy mind makes for a happy life!

Chapter 3- My Mental Motivation

ToDo 1- Daily mindful moments often are missed amidst the crazy buzz of life! Making a concerted effort to incorporate daily mindful moments into our routine can serve as a powerful anchor.

So today, go outside and find a spot to pause in your neighborhood. If you can, find a garden, a koi pond, or a close park and sit down. Now, simply observe your surroundings with curiosity using your 5 senses (sight, sound, touch, smell, and taste-well, maybe not this one).

      Listen to the sounds... how do they make you feel?

      Look at the colors around you... do you have favorites?

      Feel the air movement or the sun... what emotion do you connect with this?

      Breathe deeply & smell the air?....can you associate a memory with this smell?

Write down what your senses are telling you. Do you feel more "in touch" with yourself?

_____

_____

_____

_____

_____

_____

Fall In Love with: YOURSELF!

ToDo 2-

Goal-setting can be overwhelming but it is a fundamental aspect of personal and professional growth, providing direction and purpose. Meeting your goals becomes easier if you break them down into manageable steps and reward yourself for achieving each step along the way.

Here is a goal for this week, broken down into 4 steps with rewards, that everyone can do: <u>Volunteer 1-3 hours of your time</u> <u>OR donate resources</u> (diapers, socks, seedlings, money, etc...) <u>to support a cause you believe in.</u>

Step 4: Do it!

GO make your donation in person and check out what else they're doing.

Step 3: Make your commitment

Now, give thought to how you realistically can help in the next week. If you don't have much spare time, donating may be best - so what will you give, how will you get it, and how will you give it to them?

Step2: Discover what they need

Ask them what donations they need now OR what volunteer opportunities they have available this/next week. The organization may have this posted on their website, or you can call to speak with the volunteer/donation coordinator.

Step 1: Identify interests and causes & select an organization

Think about your personal interests and values and consider what causes mean the most to you; is it environmental conservation, animal welfare, education, homelessness, or something else? Look up, or ask friends, about local organizations that serve these interests to decide where to volunteer or donate.

Fall In Love with: YOURSELF!

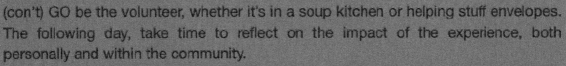

(con't) GO be the volunteer, whether it's in a soup kitchen or helping stuff envelopes. The following day, take time to reflect on the impact of the experience, both personally and within the community.

Reward: Plan a meaningful experience that nourishes the soul, such as visiting a loved one who lives farther away, participating in a special church event or revival, or taking a day trip to explore a new place. This reward acknowledges your value and love of personal growth and your ability to contribute.

(con't) If you have a flexible schedule, volunteering may be the way to go - so what day will you be there, how many hours can you give, and what is the task/job you will be doing? BOTH choices complete this goal!

Reward: Pamper yourself with a wellness treatment, treat yourself to a new journal, or buy a piece of artwork that makes your heart sing. This reward celebrates your commitment the love inside of you and encourages you to meet your goal.

Reward:
Enjoy a special activity that brings joy and relaxation, like visiting a botanical garden or local museum, or having a meal at a favorite restaurant. This reward recognizes the love you are able to share and provides a well-deserved break.

Reward:
Treat yourself to a relaxing evening doing something you enjoy, like reading this book, watching a movie, or indulging in a hobby. This reward exercises your love of self, and the importance of self-care, while encouraging reflection on your personal interests.

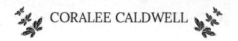

Fall In Love with: YOURSELF!

ToDo 3– Comedy therapy involves techniques that use laughter to alleviate stress and build connections with others who are in the same boat. I challenge you to find a stand-up comedy workshops (yes, they exist - look up "ComedySportz!"). If that is too much of a leap for you, then go see a live, stand-up comedy show with a friend or partner, with this caveat; make sure to find a comedian who is known for talking about topics that touch your life. Backup plan: If nothing else works, pull up a comedy special on your TV or computer and watch it with someone who is within 10 years of your age. Laughter heals the soul and is the best medicine. Laugh at yourself and love yourself!

ToDo 4– Think about your goals, professional and personal, and the manageable steps these goals could be broken down into like we did in ToDo 2. Make a personalized list of some rewards you could give yourself for achieving each milestones. Next time you're "stuck" you can come back to this list to incentivize yourself to keep moving towards the goal.

Rewards to give Myself:

Chapter 4
My Money

Let's get into the mode of finding financial fun in your 50s! This chapter invites you to venture on a delightful exploration of financial management during this significant phase of life, where wisdom intertwines with whimsy. Together, let's delve into the financial landscape of midlife and beyond, uncovering the laughter and levity that accompany it every step of the way.

As you navigate through this pivotal decade, where experience and adventure merge, it becomes imperative to approach your finances with a harmonious blend of practicality and humor. After all, what's the joy of reaching your 50s if you can't share a hearty laugh or two, particularly when it comes to money matters, along the way?

Within these pages, we'll venture on an expedition into the lighter side of money matters. From the comical missteps of budgeting blunders to the whimsical twists of retirement planning, we'll unravel the intricacies of financial management with a lighthearted touch.

Prepare to immerse yourself in the enchanting tales of splurges—moments where indulgence transcends mere financial satisfaction to evoke genuine smiles and cherished memories. These anecdotes serve as gentle reminders that, amidst the numbers and calculations, there's room for joy and frivolity in our financial journey.

So, gather your favorite financial planner, (which may be yourself) along with a generous dose of humor, and let's head into a delightful exploration of "Money Matters with Mirth."

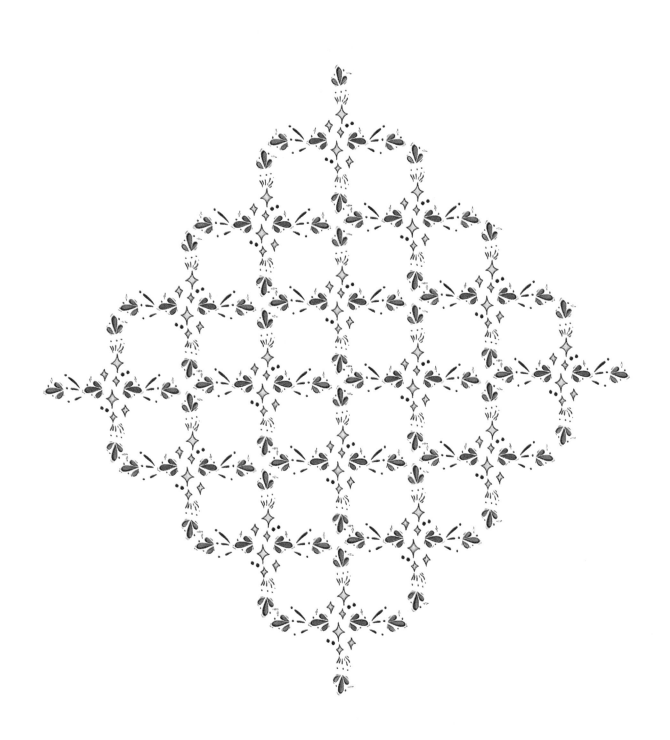

Let's Learn About It

Financial challenges

- Retirement planning: Many women in their 50s may face the challenge of inadequate retirement savings. They may have to catch up on contributions to ensure a comfortable retirement.

- Budgeting: Balancing expenses while saving for retirement and possibly supporting children or aging parents can be challenging. Women in their 50s may need to reassess their budget and cut unnecessary expenses.

- Healthcare costs: As individuals age, healthcare expenses tend to increase. Women in their 50s may need to account for rising healthcare costs in their financial plans.

- Debt management: Women in their 50s may still have lingering debt, such as mortgages, student loans, or credit card debt. Managing and reducing debt before retirement becomes crucial.

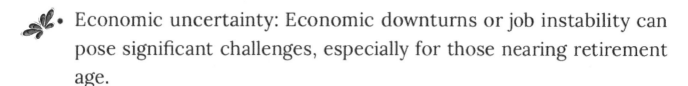
- Economic uncertainty: Economic downturns or job instability can pose significant challenges, especially for those nearing retirement age.

- Divorce and creating your financial plan: Finding yourself on your own for the first time in a long time, comes with a new set of challenges but it is also an opportunity to create your financial path.

Financial opportunities

- Investment opportunities: Women in their 50s can choose to diversify their investment portfolios and take advantage of higher-reward investments to potentially grow their wealth. Be mindful that you hire a trusted financial advisor if you choose this path.

- Career advancement: Some women may find themselves at a stage in their careers where they have opportunities for salary increases or promotions, leading to increased earning potential.

- Empty nest: With children leaving home, women in their 50s may find themselves with more disposable income to allocate toward savings and investments.

- Financial education: There are numerous resources available for financial education, empowering women to take control of their financial futures through learning about investing, budgeting, and retirement planning.

Navigating financial journeys with humor and confidence

- Embrace learning: Approach financial education with curiosity and a sense of humor. There's no shame in seeking knowledge and asking questions.

- Celebrate progress: Recognize and celebrate small victories along the way, whether it's paying off debt, increasing savings, or making smart investment decisions.

- Seek support: Surround yourself with a supportive network of friends, family, or financial advisors who can offer guidance and encouragement.

- Find the funny: Use humor as a tool to alleviate financial stress and keep a positive mindset, even in challenging times.

- Stay flexible: Be willing to adapt your financial plans as circumstances change, and maintain a sense of flexibility and resilience.

In our 50s, we can approach our financial journeys with humor, confidence, and a proactive mindset by acknowledging both the challenges and opportunities. One way we can advance our financial literacy involves exploring resources such as books, websites, and continuing education classes focused on finance and investment management. Websites like Investopedia and The Balance offer comprehensive guides and articles covering various financial topics, while books like *Rich Dad Poor Dad* by Robert Kiyosaki and *The Total Money Makeover* by Dave Ramsey provide valuable insights into building wealth and financial freedom. Seeking advice from professionals such as financial advisors, certified financial planners (CFPs), and fiduciaries can also prove beneficial. These professionals can offer personalized guidance and strategies tailored to our individual financial goals and circumstances. Additionally, managing our finances independently entails creating a budget, tracking expenses, and exploring investment opportunities such as retirement accounts and stocks. Utilizing financial management tools and apps like Mint or Personal Capital can help streamline the process and provide a clear overview of our financial health. By taking proactive steps and leveraging available resources, we, in our 50s, can gain control over our finances and work towards a secure and prosperous future.

What They Didn't Tell Us

Oh my, navigating the world of finances is like setting off on an epic journey, full of twists and tales of triumph, trepidation, and the occasional comedy of errors, including perhaps not even knowing where we are going at times! As we explore a bit further into the realm of financial planning, mishaps, and the art of balancing indulgence with vigilance, we uncover stories that resonate with the shared experience of managing money. (Pseudonyms have been used).

Take Elena, who, amidst her busy life, misplaced her utility bill, only to remember about it when receiving a reminder call for the overdue payment. Chuckling at her oversight, she set up automatic payments, deciding that her memory could no longer be trusted with the due dates of her bills.

Retirement planning—dispelling myths

Retirement planning often carries with it misconceptions, such as the belief that one can never save enough to retire comfortably. Yet, the story of Alice, who started her retirement savings late in her career, challenges this notion. By maximizing her contributions and investing wisely, Alice demonstrates that it's never too late to start preparing for retirement. She humorously notes, "Retirement is like a surprise party planned by your future self. Make sure it's a party you want to attend."

Another common myth is the idea that retirement means the end of productivity. However, many find it to be the beginning of pursuing passions and hobbies with vigor. Janet, for instance, turned her gardening hobby into a small business post-retirement, proving that retirement can indeed be a fruitful phase of life. A friend of mine started a school for disadvantaged children which has become a huge success. Heck, I even started writing books just like this one in "retirement."

The art and challenge of budgeting

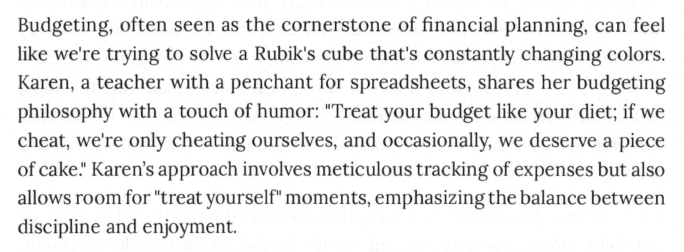

Budgeting, often seen as the cornerstone of financial planning, can feel like we're trying to solve a Rubik's cube that's constantly changing colors. Karen, a teacher with a penchant for spreadsheets, shares her budgeting philosophy with a touch of humor: "Treat your budget like your diet; if we cheat, we're only cheating ourselves, and occasionally, we deserve a piece of cake." Karen's approach involves meticulous tracking of expenses but also allows room for "treat yourself" moments, emphasizing the balance between discipline and enjoyment.

If we haven't been budgeting or involved in household budgeting before, fear not! It's never too late to start. Budgeting is like giving ourselves a financial education, helping us understand where our money goes, how much we're spending on various expenses, and where we can potentially save. We can find examples and templates for budgeting online, through apps, or even by consulting with financial professionals. Understanding the numbers and being actively involved in budgeting is crucial because it gives us a clear picture of our financial health and empowers us to make informed decisions about our spending, saving, and investing.

Effective budgeting also means being prepared for the unexpected. When Mia faced a sudden car repair bill, her "rainy day" fund turned what could have been a financial disaster into a minor hiccup. Her advice? "Always expect the unexpected, and if it doesn't happen, we've got ourselves a surprise savings account!" By actively participating in budgeting and setting aside funds for emergencies, we not only protect ourselves from financial setbacks but also gain peace of mind knowing that we're prepared for whatever life throws our way.

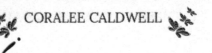

Let's Laugh About It

Once upon a time, there was a woman who decided to divorce her husband. It wasn't because he left the toilet seat up one too many times or because he had a secret collection of socks under the bed. No, she just felt like she needed a change.

So, she packed her bags, bid farewell to her ex and his sock collection, and began her new life as a single woman. Little did she know, this divorce would lead her to an unexpected and lucrative career passion.

At first, she was a little lost. She spent her days binge-watching Netflix and eating ice cream straight from the tub. But one day, while scrolling through job listings online, she stumbled upon an ad for a professional wine taster.

"Perfect!" she exclaimed, realizing that her love for wine (and perhaps her need for a distraction) could turn into a paying gig.

She promptly enrolled in wine-tasting classes, honed her palate, and soon found herself with a prestigious job as a wine critic for a renowned magazine. Her divorce turned out to be the best thing that ever happened to her career-wise.

Now, she travels the world, sipping on the finest wines, and getting paid handsomely to do so. And as for her ex? Well, last she heard, he was still searching for his missing socks, while she was too busy living her best life to even think about him

Financial mishaps: A comedy of errors

Picture Sara, a diligent saver, and a meticulous planner. One day, she decides to log into her online banking account, only to realize she has forgotten her password. After several failed attempts and getting locked out, she calls customer service, only to be reminded that her security question is "What is your favorite movie?" A question she chose a decade ago. Hours later, after guessing every movie from "The Godfather" to "Frozen," she remembers: It's "Shrek 2." This humorous anecdote serves as a gentle reminder of the importance of keeping track of our financial access codes, perhaps in a more memorable manner.

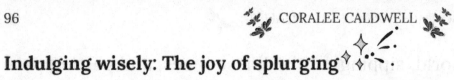

Indulging wisely: The joy of splurging

Responsible financial planning does not mean perpetual self-denial. Stories of well-deserved splurges highlight the importance of balancing saving with spending on joys that enrich life. Take Rachel, for example, who saved diligently to afford a dream vacation to Italy. Her trip was not only a celebration of her financial discipline but also a reminder that "Money is a tool for creating joy, not just a number in a bank account."

Similarly, Sophia's story of saving for a luxury handbag illustrates that indulgences, when planned and saved for, can bring immense satisfaction without guilt. She quips, "Buying that handbag felt like giving a high-five to my financially responsible self."

Through tales of forgotten passwords, budgeting escapades, retirement planning adventures, and well-deserved splurges, the journey of financial planning is revealed to be a blend of discipline, humor, and occasional indulgence. These stories underscore the importance of approaching finances with a proactive and positive mindset, proving that with the right balance, managing money can be both a responsible duty and a source of joy. Remember, the path to financial wisdom is not just about the numbers; it's about crafting a story of financial success that includes laughter, learning, and, yes, even a luxury handbag or two!

How to Engage and Embrace the Changes

Engaging with change, especially as we step into our 50s, feels like navigating a new city without a map. It's exciting, and sometimes a bit daunting, but it is also full of possibilities. This chapter in life often prompts us to reassess our financial landscapes, aiming to secure comfort, stability, and perhaps a sprinkle of adventure for the days ahead. Let's explore embracing these changes confidently, focusing on organizing financial documents, managing accounts with ease, and understanding the invaluable role of a financial advisor.

Organizing financial documents: Your roadmap to clarity

Imagine organizing your financial documents as assembling pieces of a puzzle. Once organized, they form a clear picture of your financial standing and direction. Ah, the joys of knowing where everything is! Here are some practical tips to get you started:

 • Consolidate and categorize: Start by collecting all your financial documents, including bank statements, investment records, insurance policies, wills, and any debt-related documents.

Categorize them in a way that makes sense to you: by type, by account, or by date.

- Go digital: In our digital era, creating electronic copies of your documents saves space and reduces clutter. Use a scanner or a smartphone scanning app. Store these documents on a secure cloud service, but also keep a physical backup on an external hard drive.

- Stay current: Establish a monthly ritual to update your documents. Shred old bills or statements and replace them with new ones. This practice keeps your files manageable and ensures you have the most current information at hand.

- Emergency access: Make sure a trusted family member or friend knows where to find these documents and how to access them in case of an emergency. Maybe even make them copies. This foresight acts as a beacon of light during unforeseen storms.

Managing accounts with ease: The joy of simplification

Managing multiple accounts across different platforms can feel overwhelming, and simplification is the key!

- Consolidate accounts: Review all your bank and retirement accounts. If you have multiple accounts of the same type across different institutions, consider consolidating them. This reduces mental clutter and may also decrease fees.

- Automate payments: Set up automatic payments for recurring bills and savings. Automation ensures you never miss a payment and helps avoid late fees. It also simplifies tracking your monthly money flow.

• Use financial management tools: Embrace technology by using financial management apps or software. These tools help track your spending, manage your budget, and provide insights into your financial habits.

The benefits of working with a financial advisor

Paddling in the financial waters of your 50s can be complex, but you don't have to do it alone. Working with a financial advisor offers clarity, direction, and peace of mind. Here are some benefits and success stories to inspire you:

• Customized financial strategies: Financial advisors develop personalized strategies that align with your goals, be it securing a comfortable retirement, funding a passion project, or leaving a legacy for your loved ones.

• Expertise and experience: Advisors bring a wealth of knowledge and experience, helping you avoid common pitfalls and seize opportunities you might have overlooked.

• Accountability and support: They act as your financial coach, encouraging you to stay on track toward your goals and making adjustments as necessary.

Success stories

Kelly's encore career: At 52, Kelly felt lost navigating her retirement options. Her advisor's guidance revealed she could afford to retire from her corporate job and pursue her dream of starting a small bakery. Her advisor helped her budget for this transition, ensuring her savings supported her new venture without sacrificing her retirement goals.

Sophia's investment triumph: Sophia always feared the stock market. Her financial advisor demystified investing, explaining risks and rewards in simple terms. With a tailored investment plan, she watched her portfolio grow, providing financial stability and confidence she never thought possible.

Maria's debt-free journey: After a divorce left her finances in disarray, Maria worked with a financial advisor to create a debt repayment plan. Through budget adjustments and strategic financial decisions, she celebrated being debt-free within three years, a milestone she credits to expert advice and personalized support.

Embracing change in our 50s with organization, simplification, and expert guidance can transform financial challenges into opportunities for growth and security. Organizing your financial documents gives you a clear overview of your financial standing while simplifying account management streamlines your financial life. Partnering with a financial advisor unlocks paths to stability and fulfillment you might not have discovered on your own. As we travel through this exciting chapter of life, let's remember that with the right tools and support, we're not just preparing for the future; we're actively shaping it into a journey we look forward to with confidence and anticipation.

Chapter 4- My Money

ToDo 1- Financial Clarity Collage

Create a banner collage representing your current financial situation and future goals. This collage will motivate you and remind you of your targets.

Materials needed: white paper (or colored), twine/string, magazines, photographs, or printed images (think internet!), glue/glue sticks, tape, markers or colored pencils/pens for labeling.

Instructions:
- Start by considering your financial goals, such as retirement, travel, starting a business, or achieving debt freedom.
- Search through your materials. Select images and words that depict your 1. current financial situation, 2. your goals, and 3. the steps needed to achieve them.
- If you are fancy, cut your papers into a triangle or pennant shapes, but feel completely free to use the rectangular shape it comes in. Assemble these images and words on your paper(s)-use as many as you need, creating a banner collage that illustrates your path to financial clarity and freedom. Tape them onto a long string like you are decorating it for a birthday party.
- Hang your collage where you can see it every day, (bedroom, bathroom, walk-in-closet-type girls!), to keep your financial goals at the forefront of your mind.

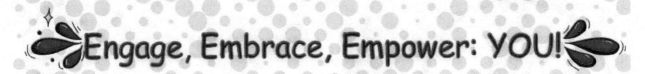

Engage, Embrace, Empower: YOU!

ToDo 2- Digital Decluttering & Organization

Spend time organizing your financial documents digitally. This will minimize clutter, increase security, and streamline your finance management.

You will need a computer or almost any digital device and a scanner or smartphone with a scanning app - free scanner apps already on your phone...

"Notes" on iPhones
1. Open Notes and select create a new one.
2. Tap the Camera icon mid-screen
3. Tap Scan Documents
4. Place your document in view of the camera.
5. If your device is in Auto mode, hold your phone steady until it automatically scan the document for you. If not, click the round button to take the picture.
6. Tap Keep Scan- You can now just point the camera at your next document page, but don't forget to save them all (step 7) when you're done!
7. Tap Save. These docs are now inside your Notes app. You can name them, move them to "Files" or send them to store wherever you'd like.

"Android Scanner" on Android phones
1. Open the "Google Drive" app on your Android device.
2. Tap the "+" (plus) button at the bottom right corner of the screen.
3. Select "Scan" from the options that appear.
4. Position your device's camera over the document you want to scan.
5. Adjust your scanned document. ...
6. Tap Done
7. Create your own file name/title
8. Save to your digital device (or cloud storage)

Instructions:
- Allocate 2–3 hours to do this. Start by collecting all your physical financial documents for digital conversion. (Bank, health, insurance, etc.)
- Scan each document, naming them clearly and logically (e.g., "2024_TaxDocuments," "HealthInsurance_Policy").
- Upload these documents to your selected secure cloud service and save backup copies on an external hard drive.
- Organize the files into new, well-labeled folders and remove any old, outdated ones.
- Choose one day/date per month and set a reminder to continue updating your documents. This will keep your digital financial life organized and up-to-date.

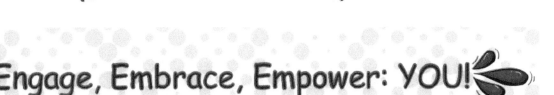

Engage, Embrace, Empower: YOU!

ToDo 3- Journal on Financial Changes & Goals

Prompt: "As I navigate my 50s and beyond, how have my financial priorities shifted? What new goals have emerged, and how can I align my current financial practices to support these new or shifted goals?"Consider the steps you can take to embrace these changes positively and proactively.

Instructions:

- Choose a quiet, comfortable spot for reflection without interruptions.
- Think about the prompt before writing. Reflect on the financial changes you've experienced, the achievements you've made since age 45, and the financial goals you're striving for.
- Finish up your entry by committing to 1-2 actions you'll take next month to advance towards your goals.

Engage, Embrace, Empower: YOU!

Falling in Love with Your Money

Falling in love with your money isn't just about hoarding wealth or constantly checking your bank balance. It's about forming a healthy, joyful relationship with your finances, understanding where your money is going, and realizing the freedom and security that financial responsibility can bring. This perspective on money management—seeing it as a form of self-care and a pathway to fulfilling your dreams—can transform not just your bank account, but your entire life.

The joy of financial freedom

Imagine waking up every day knowing you have the financial freedom to do what you love, whether that's traveling, pursuing hobbies, or spending time with loved ones, without the worry of financial constraints. This isn't a far-fetched dream but a reality for those who've embraced financial responsibility and planning, especially for women who have historically faced challenges in achieving financial independence.

Success stories of financial independence

Take, for instance, Linda, a woman in her early 60s who began her journey to financial freedom in her 30s. Linda focused on saving a significant portion of her income, investing wisely, and living below her means. Today, she enjoys a comfortable retirement, traveling the world and engaging in activities she's passionate about, from art classes to volunteering. Linda's story, shared by financial educator Jean Chatzky in her book *Women with Money* (Chatzky, 2019), illustrates the power of consistent, long-term financial planning and saving.

Similarly, Emma's tale, featured in *The Financial Diet* by Chelsea Fagan and Lauren Ver Hage (Fagan & Ver Hage, 2018), showcases how a strategic approach to debt repayment and savings enabled her to launch her dream business in her 50s. Emma's commitment to financial health allowed her to transition from feeling overwhelmed by money to using it as a tool to achieve her dreams.

The newly divorced woman: After years of marriage, Emma finds herself newly divorced and facing a blank slate. While she mourns the end of her marriage, she also sees it as an opportunity for a fresh start, especially when it comes to her finances.

Emma has always been a bit of a free spirit when it comes to money, never really paying much attention to her budget or saving for the future. But now, with newfound independence, she knows she has to get serious about her financial future. She starts by creating a detailed budget, tracking every penny she spends, and identifying areas where she can cut back. She also opens a retirement account and sets up automatic contributions, determined to build a nest egg for herself.

But Emma doesn't stop there. She also enrolls in financial literacy classes and starts reading books on investing and wealth building. She even begins side hustles to increase her income and accelerate her savings.

As the months go by, Emma's diligence pays off. She watches her savings grow, her debt shrink, and her confidence in her financial future soar. And while her divorce has been a difficult chapter in her life, Emma knows that it has also been the catalyst for her newfound financial success.

The couple who forgot to save for retirement: Meet Tom and Lisa, a couple who have spent their entire lives living in the moment, never giving much thought to their financial future. They are content to enjoy life as it comes, without worrying about what tomorrow might bring.

But as they approach their 50s, reality begins to set in. They realize that they have not saved nearly enough for retirement and are now facing the prospect of working well into their golden years. Determined to turn things around, Tom and Lisa sit down together to devise a plan. They start by cutting back on unnecessary expenses, downsizing their lifestyle, and redirecting those savings into retirement accounts.

They also seek the help of a financial advisor, who helps them create a personalized retirement plan tailored to their goals and circumstances. Together, they explore investment options and strategies to maximize their savings potential. It isn't easy, and there are sacrifices along the way, but Tom and Lisa are committed to securing their financial future. They pick up extra shifts, take on freelance work, and even sell some of their belongings to boost their savings.

As they watch their retirement accounts grow, Tom and Lisa feel a sense of pride and accomplishment. They have taken control of their financial destiny and are now on track to enjoy a comfortable retirement together.

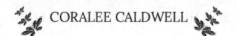

And while they may have started late, they know that it is never too late to start planning for the future.

Embracing financial self-care and finding joy in money management

Financial self-care involves regular check-ins with your finances, setting and revisiting financial goals, and educating yourself about money management. It means making informed decisions about spending, saving, and investing, ensuring that your financial actions align with your long-term goals and values.

Our beliefs about money significantly impact our financial decisions and behaviors. By transforming negative money beliefs into positive affirmations and actions, we can develop a healthier relationship with our finances.

Finding joy in managing your money might sound paradoxical, especially if you've experienced financial stress. However, the process of taking control of your finances, setting goals, and seeing progress can be incredibly rewarding and empowering. Celebrating small victories, such as paying off a credit card or reaching a savings milestone, reinforces positive financial behaviors.

Deriving pleasure from saving and investing, rather than just spending, is key to long-term financial well-being and happiness. Viewing money management as a form of self-respect and taking steps toward securing your future happiness and well-being is crucial for being able to enjoy managing your money.

Steps to fall in love with your money

- Understand your money: Keep track of where your money goes each month. Use apps or spreadsheets to monitor your spending and savings. Awareness is the first step towards change.

• Set clear financial goals: Whether it's saving for retirement, building an emergency fund, or paying off debt, having **S**pecific, **M**easurable, **A**chievable, **R**elevant, and **Ti**me-bound (SMART) goals, can guide your financial decisions and actions (Mind Tools, 2023).

• Educate yourself: Invest time in learning about personal finance, whether through books, podcasts, or online courses. Knowledge is power, and understanding financial principles can help you make informed decisions.

• Celebrate progress: Acknowledge and celebrate every financial milestone, no matter how small. These celebrations reinforce positive behaviors and keep you motivated.

• Seek professional advice: A financial advisor can offer personalized advice tailored to your unique financial situation and goals. They can also provide accountability and encouragement on your journey to financial well-being.

• Cultivate a positive money mindset: Challenge and replace negative beliefs about money with positive affirmations. Remind yourself that you're capable of achieving financial success and that money is a tool to help you realize your dreams.

Falling in love with your money is about more than just numbers; it's about creating a life that aligns with your values and dreams. By embracing financial responsibility and finding joy in the process, you can achieve financial freedom and live a life filled with passion and purpose.

Chapter 4- My Money

ToDo 1- Snapshot of Financial Net Worth

Figuring out your personal net worth is probably easier than you think! The purpose is to give you a clear, immediate view of where you stand financially.

1st- Gather your most current budget & financial statements, plus have access to the financial documents you recently digitized (and any of those you didn't).

2nd- Choose a website you trust (the most!) that has a Net Worth Calculator.
- I suggest The FDIC- https://playmoneysmart.fdic.gov/tools/22
- Or AARP- https://www.aarp.org/money/investing/net_worth_calculator/
- Or Nerd Wallet- https://www.nerdwallet.com/article/finance/net-worth-calculator

3rd- Read the page and scroll down to the Net Worth Calculator. Fill in the required information, and Voilà aka Whalla! Now you know…

You might ♡ the outcome, or you might not be so thrilled :-(. Whatever your initial reaction is, **LOVE** on yourself for even making it to this step. More than half of all Americans have no clue what a personal net worth even is! This financial reality check allows you to make informed decisions that you WILL♡ going forward.

Fall In Love with: YOURSELF!

ToDo 2- Plan your Ultimate Dream SLURGE

Transform those abstract desires into achievable goals!

Identify something luxurious or highly desirable you've always wanted to do or buy, but considered out of reach. Write it out in large letters here.

My ultimate dream splurge is:

Now, let's break down the financial steps for you to achieve this goal.

Overall cost/budget: $_____

Potential sources of extra income: _____

_____

_____

Break down the finances into 3-4 milestones:

First timeline savings goal 1 date: _____ and $_____

Timeline savings goal date 2: _____ and $_____

Timeline savings goal date 3: _____ and $_____

Final timeline savings goal date 4: _____ and

MY DREAM SPLURGE DATE:

Fall In Love with: YOURSELF!

ToDo 3- Financial Comedy Journal

Grab a new notebook or order a special "journal" online. (Most are less that $8.00 on Amazon.). Title it "Financial Faux Pas" and place it in your nightstand or your underwear drawer.   It is now your financial comedy journal where you record and reminisce over your past amusing and ironic experiences related to money. Whether it's a humorous mistake, a funny coincidence, or a weird habit, whenever you think of it, write it down. Laughing about your financial blunders or *oddities* promotes a positive attitude towards personal finance, making it more enjoyable and less daunting. Here are some examples…

11/16/20xx
-At some point in time I used a $50 dollar bill as a bookmark in "The Scarlet Letter." Last week, I let my daughter Jessi use my beloved copy for her English class. Today she came home and ran straight up to me,

01/07/20xx
-Today I stopped by Goodwill on my way home because I needed a "new" pair of gardening jeans. Believe it or not, after trying some on, I found a pair that fit, so I paid and went home. This evening, when I put them on to

threw her arms around me and said, "Thanks Mom! You're the best!" I was completely confused until she told me what happened. YES, I tried to get my $50 back, but we all know how that went over with a teenager!!!

go out to the backyard garden, I put my hands in the pocket and FOUND $20.00! Lucky me!

Fall In Love with: YOURSELF!

07/24/20xx

-I always pay Ben his allowance on Saturday mornings, so today I did that... so I thought. Turns out, I sent Pastor Ben $15.00 instead of my son. OMGosh was I embarrassed when he sent me a text saying "Is this just a random blessing or a mistake?"

All these money sending apps can get so confusing!

12/26/20xx

-Tried to make some extra Christmas cash this year by selling old stuff we had in boxes in the garage. I sold a whole box full of old cups, mugs, and steins no one has ever used and made a quick $80.00. When Trey came home and I

proudly showed him the money I made he flipped out... How was I to know that those old beer steins were worth about $100 each???????
:-(

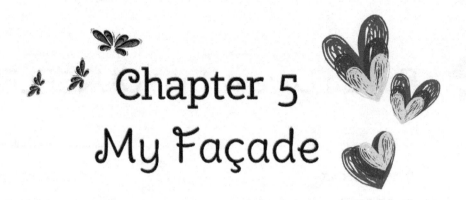

Chapter 5
My Façade

Oh, the trials and tribulations of navigating fashion and beauty faux pas in your 50s! Here, we wholeheartedly embrace the raucous laughter that accompanies this rollercoaster journey of aging gracefully (or, let's face it, not always so gracefully) in the ever-evolving world of style and beauty.

Fashion and beauty blunders are practically a rite of passage during this dynamic decade of life! From the occasional wardrobe malfunction to those infamous makeup mishaps, we've all experienced these moments when questioning our fashion choices and beauty routines. But fear not, my fellow 50-something, in these moments of embarrassing hilarity, we discover a sense of camaraderie and an appreciation for the wonderfully imperfect beings that we are.

Venturing into the ever-changing trends of fashion, often a delightful recycling of past styles with each new generation's twist—sometimes leaves us scratching our heads and rummaging through our closets in pursuit of the ever-elusive "perfect outfit." What even is perfection anyway? And, let's not forget the exhilarating highs and occasional lows of wardrobe wonders and woes. Who hasn't pondered whether they can still rock those skinny jeans and short shorts?

But it's not all about clothing; let's not overlook the beauty regimes and rituals, where the mirror becomes a comedic accomplice in some cases. You know what I mean! Oh, the stories to be told. From those hilarious botched DIY haircuts (seriously, why do we think we can trim our bangs?)

to experimenting with new skincare products that promise to turn back the clock but instead leave us looking like a tomato! Through it all, we share a good old laugh at our own expense and revel in the utter beauty of imperfection!

And then there are the accessory accidents where style meets comedy in the most unexpected ways. Whether it's gracefully (or not) tripping over our heels or realizing a bit too late that our statement necklace is more of a "What was I thinking?" statement, we embrace the laughter of these moments and proudly wear them as badges of honor.

So gather your favorite fashion faux pas and your trusty tube of mascara, (because let's be real, mascara is usually the one thing that never lets us down—unless we decide to go swimming and realize it wasn't waterproof after, all...but let's not digress). When it comes to navigating the wild and wonderful world of fashion and beauty in your 50s, one thing is crystal clear: The most valuable accessory is indeed a good sense of humor.

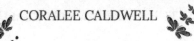
Let's Learn About It

So we know fashion and beauty trends continually evolve, influenced by cultural shifts, technological advancements, and societal norms. Staying abreast of these trends is influenced by various factors, such as societal values, cultural influences, and individual preferences. This era marks a time for authentic self-expression and personal reinvention, with confidence. We may encounter challenges finding their way through these shifts, which can be simultaneously exciting and daunting. Exploring the intricacies of fashion trends, and beauty standards, and the empowering journey of embracing personal style and grooming confidence can be exhilarating. However, it's essential to recognize that personal style and grooming play pivotal roles, not only for outward appearance but also for conveying unique self-expression and self-confidence.

There has been a notable shift towards inclusivity and diversity within the fashion and beauty industries, driven by public pressure and more women voicing their preferences and talking about what is important to them. This inclusivity empowers all women by validating their diverse experiences and celebrating their individuality. The rise of social media and digital platforms

has democratized fashion and beauty, providing us with unprecedented access to style inspirations and beauty tips. Much has changed!

Personal style has created a movement that enables us to communicate our identity, values, and aspirations through appearance. Cultivating a distinct personal style can be liberating and transformative, boosting confidence and honing a greater sense of empowerment. It transcends mere trend-following; it's about authentically embracing individuality. By curating a wardrobe that resonates with your unique aesthetic, we can feel confident in our choices, regardless of societal expectations.

From beauty routines to hairstyling techniques, prioritizing self-care and self-love is right at the top of the list. Investing in quality skincare products and embracing natural beauty become integral components of grooming routines, enhancing self-confidence and overall well-being.

Embracing self-expression and self-assured personal style is an empowering journey. It invites women to embrace authenticity, celebrate individuality, and cultivate confidence from within. Whether experimenting with bold fashion statements or refining skincare routines, the focus is placed on celebrating diversity, embracing self-expression, and redefining standards of style and beauty for women in their 50s and beyond!

Recent scientific studies emphasize the need for tailored skincare routines that adapt to changing skin conditions at different life stages (Wrightman & Sissons, 2022). During teenage years, managing acne and oiliness is crucial, alongside establishing good skincare habits like gentle cleansing, moisturizing, and sun protection. As we progress into our 20s and 30s, skin care needs to evolve with the emergence of fine lines and wrinkles due to declining collagen production. Scientifically studied interventions such as antioxidants and retinoids help mitigate these effects. Sun protection remains vital throughout adulthood to prevent sunburn and reduce the risk of skin cancer. Incorporating these practices helps maintain healthy skin as we age.

In our 50s, skincare becomes even more critical due to hormonal fluctuations and decreased collagen production. Dermatologists recommend a comprehensive regimen including gentle cleansing, moisturizing, and targeted treatments like retinoids to address fine lines and age spots. Sunscreen is essential for daily protection. For fashion advice, we can seek inspiration from fashion magazines, blogs, and social media tailored to different age groups.

Decluttering our wardrobe involves letting go of outdated items like shoulder pads, and focusing on timeless pieces like blazers, trousers, dresses, and accessories. Common sense guidelines include investing in high-quality, flattering pieces and embracing individual style preferences. Fashion post-50 should celebrate personal style and confidence, guided by skincare best practices and practical dressing tips.

Take heed that true style begins with self-assurance and radiates from within while embracing authenticity at every stage of life. Cheers to the beauty of authenticity!

What They Didn't Tell Us

There is a lot to share about the humorous side of fashion and beauty in your 50s! Let's explore this delightful time where fashion faux pas and beauty mishaps take center stage. We've all had our share of experiences, from the dreaded mismatched outfits to the DIY hair coloring experiment that went hilariously awry.

Imagine this scenario: You're preparing for a night out, feeling confident in your chosen attire, (that you picked out in your dark closet), only to realize midway through the evening that the red top you chose is dark pink and clashes terribly with your bright orange skirt, which wasn't the look you intended. Cue the awkward shuffling and the sheepish apologies as you attempt to pass off your fashion blunder as avant-garde style.

And then there's the unforgettable DIY hair coloring disaster—a tale as old as time. You thought you could save a few bucks by dyeing your hair at home, only to discover that the result is more fluorescent than fashionable. Suddenly, you're sporting a vibrant hue reminiscent of a tropical bird, rather than the chic look you envisioned. Lesson learned: leave hair color to the professionals next time.

But it's not just about fashion faux pas; it's also about navigating the ever-evolving world of fashion trends. As women in our 50s, we're no strangers to the excitement of discovering the latest styles and embracing new trends. However, keeping up with these fleeting fads can sometimes feel like a never-ending game of catch-up. From oversized blazers to neon hues, each season brings its own set of challenges and delights. We find ourselves torn between staying in our budget and on-trend, but still staying true to our style, often resulting in a mishmash of all. But hey, fashion is all about experimentation, right? So, why not embrace the chaos and rock those statement sleeves like nobody's business? Create your style, be unique!

Of course, no discussion of fashion and beauty in your 50s would be complete without delving into the quest for the perfect anti-aging potion—a journey filled with more twists and turns than a soap opera plotline.

We've all fallen prey to the allure of skincare products promising to reverse the signs of aging and restore youthful radiance. From serums to creams to masks, we've tried them all in pursuit of the elusive fountain of youth. And while some products live up to their promises, others leave us questioning whether we've inadvertently become subjects in a scientific experiment gone wrong. Try to avoid falling into the trap of the elusive elixirs and embrace the privilege of growing older, marked by those lines and wrinkles with the realization that beauty is far deeper than what your skin looks like.

Now, let's not overlook the realm of makeup mishaps—a universal experience for women everywhere. We have spoken about the dreaded mascara smudge already but what about the foundation line that's visible from space? Maybe no one has told you so, but the make-up we wore in our 20 to 30s is not the same kind we should be wearing in our 50s. It has to change, or we'll have our fair share of beauty blunders. But hey, laughter is indeed the best medicine, so why not chuckle at our imperfections and perhaps consider dropping the makeup once and for all? It would certainly make life a lot easier.

Finally, we come to the comical aspects of attempting to maintain a stylish and put-together appearance. Ah, yes, the struggle is real, from wrestling with stubborn zippers to attempting to walk gracefully in sky-high heels, there's never a dull moment in the pursuit of sartorial perfection. Sometimes comfort is the better choice. Rock your style!

But amidst the chaos and laughter, there's a sense of camaraderie and understanding that perfection is overrated. After all, it's the quirks that make us beautifully unique, flaws and all. So, let's embrace the humor in our fashion and beauty mishaps, knowing that we're all in this together. After all, life's too short to take ourselves too seriously, especially when it comes to fashion and beauty in your 50s.

Let's Laugh About It

In the circus of fashion and beauty, which is how I like to refer to it, where trends appear and vanish in the blink of an eye, it's easy to get swept up in the glitz and glam, trying to mimic what the cool kids—or more recently, internet influencers—are doing. This journey, filled with mishaps and misadventures, often leaves us with stories more amusing than stylish. Let me share a few of my own experiences, which I hope will not only make you laugh but also remind you that it's perfectly okay to find humor in the quest to stay trendy.

The great makeup misadventure

Once, fueled by optimism and enchanted by a YouTube makeup guru who made it look as simple as spreading butter on toast, I set out to follow a makeup tutorial called "The Ultimate Glow Summer Look." I laid out my barely touched makeup collection, ready to morph into the radiant goddess the tutorial promised I'd become.

Trouble appeared when I couldn't tell the concealer from the foundation. They looked alarmingly alike but acted very differently in my unskilled hands. Still, I didn't give up, blending with the determination of a child building a sandcastle, convinced it was going to be a masterpiece.

The eyeshadow part followed. "Blend the coral hue into your crease for a pop of color," the guru advised. Calling it a "pop" was putting it mildly. It was more like an explosion, turning my eyelids into a dramatic sunset that could signal the end of days. The real challenge, however, was the liquid eyeliner. Despite being labeled as foolproof, it was anything but. My attempts at a sleek cat-eye morphed into a style best described as raccoon-chic—a trend I was sure wouldn't catch on.

In the end, the promised radiant goddess was nowhere to be found. Instead, I resembled someone who had lost a fight with a box of crayons—a vibrant but humbling reminder that makeup tutorials might not be my forte.

Jeans: The unforgiving foe

Moving on to another episode in my epic fashion journey: the jeans debacle. Jeans, that timeless staple supposed to flatter your figure, except when they don't! Driven by nostalgia, I dug out a pair of jeans from my 20s, a memento from an era when low-rise ruled, and comfort took a backseat.

Convinced they would still fit, I took on the Herculean task of wriggling into them. The process felt like being fitted for medieval armor but with more grunting and less dignity. With every shimmy and jump, I battled the denim, determined to win. The jeans, however, resisted, clinging to my thighs as stubbornly as a koala to a tree.

The fight with the zipper was an epic in its own right. It demanded strategic breathing, akin to a yoga class, and a level of pulling and tugging that would suit a medieval torture chamber. When the zipper finally gave in, it was a hollow victory. The denim encased me so tightly that sitting became an impossible dream, and taking a full breath was out of the question.

Standing there, immobilized, I couldn't help but laugh at the sheer absurdity. The jeans that once epitomized my youth now felt like a denim straitjacket, a humorous nudge that maybe some past relics are best left behind.

Lessons learned

These fashion and beauty misadventures, as embarrassing as they were, serve as comedic reminders that chasing perfection is futile. In our quest to be trendy, it's easy to overlook that the blunders and bloopers are what make the journey unforgettable. So, the next time you end up smeared in makeup that bears no resemblance to the tutorial, or trapped in an item of clothing that seemed like a good idea at the time, remember to laugh. Fashion may be fleeting, but the joy found in laughing at oneself lasts forever.

And to those influencers who make everything look effortless: I salute you. But I'll continue to embrace my style mishaps with a good chuckle, comforted by the knowledge that in the vast landscape of fashion, there's always room for a bit of imperfection.

How to Engage and Embrace the Changes

Embrace change in your style and wardrobe—it's both exhilarating and daunting. As our lives evolve, so do our bodies, our preferences, and our needs. Whether you're navigating a significant life transition, seeking to refresh your look, or simply aiming to feel more comfortable and confident in your skin, understanding how to engage with and embrace these changes is crucial. Here, we'll explore practical tips for updating your wardrobe with versatile pieces that not only flatter your body but also align with your style. We will also look into the importance of self-confidence and self-acceptance, which underscores how feeling beautiful and stylish is achievable at any age.

Updating your wardrobe with versatile pieces

Start by evaluating what you currently own. Identify pieces you love and wear often, those that don't fit well or align with your style, and missing items that could create more versatile outfit options. This process will help you understand your style preferences and the direction you wish to take.

Let foundation pieces like a well-fitting pair of jeans, a classic blazer, versatile tops, and a little black dress serve as the cornerstone of your wardrobe. Look for high-quality materials and timeless designs that offer flexibility and longevity.

Embrace your body as it is now, recognizing its beauty and uniqueness. Choose clothing that flatters your current shape, focusing on pieces that accentuate your best features. Whether it's a tailored coat that cinches your waist or pants that elongate your legs, selecting the right fit can dramatically enhance your appearance and comfort.

While basics are essential, including some statement pieces like a bold jacket, unique accessories, or eye-catching shoes can express your personality and add excitement to your outfits. These items can make your wardrobe feel fresh and reflect your evolving style.

Don't shy away from color and pattern; they can add dimension and interest to your wardrobe. If you're hesitant, start with small, manageable doses—a vibrant scarf, a patterned blouse, or colorful footwear—and gradually work your way up to include bold colors and patterns you may not have been open to wearing before.

Always prioritize garments that feel good on your body and fit well. Clothing that restricts movement or doesn't sit right can affect your mood and confidence. Remember, the best outfits are those that you can live your life in comfortably. So, prioritize comfort.

The importance of self-confidence and self-acceptance

Actively challenge societal and self-imposed standards of beauty. Beauty is diverse, subjective, and ever-evolving. Embrace your unique features and qualities, recognizing that true style transcends age, size, and trends.

Your style should reflect your life's journey and the person you've become. Celebrating your evolution means dressing for your current self, acknowledging your experiences, and expressing your growth through your wardrobe choices.

Seek inspiration, not comparison. Look for fashion inspiration from people who resonate with your style or body type, but avoid comparing yourself to them. Use social media, magazines, and fashion blogs as sources of ideas, rather than benchmarks for beauty and success.

Don't be afraid to experiment with your style for different looks and trends. Trying new things can be a fun and enlightening process that helps you discover what makes you feel most confident and happy. Remember, fashion is about personal expression and should bring you joy.

Taking care of your body and mind can significantly impact how you feel about yourself and, consequently, how you present yourself to the world. Whether it's through nutrition, exercise, meditation, or self-pampering, find activities that boost your well-being and self-esteem. Find what works best for you.

Cultivate a positive inner dialogue and be mindful of how you talk to and about yourself. Practice speaking to yourself with kindness and compassion, focusing on your strengths and achievements. A positive self-image starts from within and is reflected in how you carry yourself and interact with the world.

Surround yourself with people who uplift and support you. A supportive community of friends, family, or like-minded individuals who encourage your self-expression and personal growth can bolster your confidence and help you navigate changes with positivity and grace.

Engaging with and embracing changes in your wardrobe and personal style can be a powerful avenue for expressing your identity and enhancing your self-confidence. By focusing on versatility, fit, and self-expression, and by practicing self-acceptance and a positive mindset, you can feel beautiful and stylish at any age. Remember, the key to navigating change is not just in adapting to the new but in celebrating the journey and the transformation it brings.

Chapter 5- My Façade

ToDo 1- Host a Wardrobe Revamp Party

Invite a group of close friends to participate in a wardrobe revamp session. Each person brings items they no longer wear or love. You might want to give some guidance based on exactly who you are inviting (# of items, types of clothing, style/ season/original price limits/etc…). Arrange a space where everyone can display their items and decorate with signs that have body-positive quotes. These can be easily found and printed right off internet pages. This party serves two purposes: It's a fun and engaging way to refresh your wardrobe with "new-to-you" pieces to try, and it fosters a supportive environment for discussing body positivity, style preferences, and to reinforce the idea that fashion is an ever-evolving journey.

ToDo 2- Style Exploration Challenge

Are you ready to shake up your style routine? Find/identify 7 accessories you like/love but do not usually wear. Cut 7 small pieces of paper and write a name for each piece down. Fold the papers and dump them all into a "fishbowl' -any bowl, or big cup will do. Each day, pull one out at random and unleash your inner fashionista. Find a clever new way to design today's outfit based on your awesome accessory, then strut your stuff! Love your newfound fun, creativity, and confidence.

Engage, Embrace, Empower: YOU!

ToDo 3– Style Evolution

How has your outer-style (clothes/makeup/hair/smell) evolved over the years? Describe its different phases, and what influenced changes (such as significant life events, shifts in personal beliefs, or inspiration from cultural trends). Finally, how do these changes reflect your personal growth and celebrate your identity?

_____

_____

_____

_____

_____

_____

_____

_____

_____

_____

_____

_____

_____

_____

_____

_____

_____

_____

Engage, Embrace, Empower: YOU!

Falling in Love With Your Style

Embracing your unique beauty in a world filled with trends and societal pressures is key. Feeling like you're drowning in the pursuit of unattainable beauty standards is as common as mistaking salt for sugar in your morning coffee. But fear not, beneath the layers of expectations lies a gem of truth: Your true beauty radiates from within, and embracing your unique style is the secret sauce to unlocking your inner glow. So, grab your favorite beverage (sans salt), sit back, and let's embark on a journey of self-love and empowerment, sprinkled with stories of women who found their confidence in reinventing their style. Oh, and we'll throw in some transformative self-care rituals, because who doesn't love a bit of pampering?

Reinventing personal style: Stories of empowerment

1. A journey to self-expression: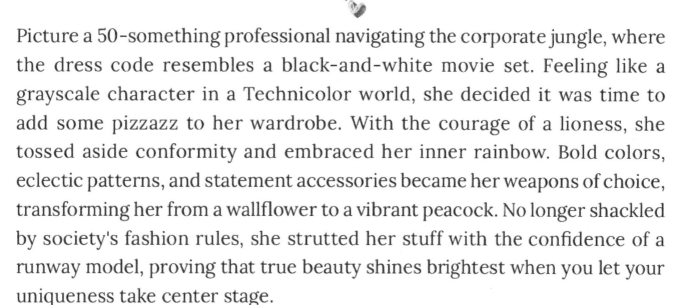

Picture a 50-something professional navigating the corporate jungle, where the dress code resembles a black-and-white movie set. Feeling like a grayscale character in a Technicolor world, she decided it was time to add some pizzazz to her wardrobe. With the courage of a lioness, she tossed aside conformity and embraced her inner rainbow. Bold colors, eclectic patterns, and statement accessories became her weapons of choice, transforming her from a wallflower to a vibrant peacock. No longer shackled by society's fashion rules, she strutted her stuff with the confidence of a runway model, proving that true beauty shines brightest when you let your uniqueness take center stage.

2. Fashion renaissance:

Now, imagine a mom of two who had resigned herself to a life of mom jeans and practical footwear. One fateful day, while browsing through a vintage clothing store, she stumbled upon a treasure trove of fashion history. With each retro find, her style blossomed like a flower in spring, shedding her frumpy cocoon to reveal a chic butterfly. Eclectic prints, vibrant colors, and timeless silhouettes became her new best friends, catapulting her from suburban mom to fashion icon. With a twinkle in her eye and a strut in her step, she embraced her quirks and imperfections, turning them into her fashion superpowers. Who knew that true style could be found in the aisles of a thrift store?

The transformative power of self-care rituals

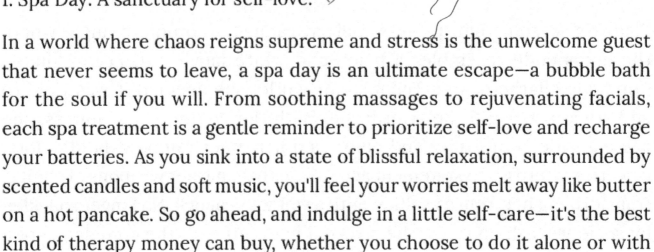

1. Spa Day: A sanctuary for self-love.

In a world where chaos reigns supreme and stress is the unwelcome guest that never seems to leave, a spa day is an ultimate escape—a bubble bath for the soul if you will. From soothing massages to rejuvenating facials, each spa treatment is a gentle reminder to prioritize self-love and recharge your batteries. As you sink into a state of blissful relaxation, surrounded by scented candles and soft music, you'll feel your worries melt away like butter on a hot pancake. So go ahead, and indulge in a little self-care—it's the best kind of therapy money can buy, whether you choose to do it alone or with some friends.

2. The simple pleasures of evening skincare.

Amidst the chaos of daily life, finding time for a little self-care can feel like searching for a needle in a haystack. Taking time out for the simple act of indulging in an evening skincare routine is a small but mighty step towards self-love. As you cleanse away the day's grime and adorn your skin with nourishing serums and moisturizers, you're not just pampering your face—you're pampering your soul. With each gentle massage and loving touch, you're sending a message to yourself: "You're worth it." So go ahead, slather on that night cream like there's no tomorrow because when it comes to self-love, there's no such thing as too much.

Falling in love with your style is not about indulgence or just following the latest trends—it's about embracing your uniqueness and celebrating the journey of self-discovery and self-expression. Through the stories of women who found their confidence in reinventing their style and the transformative power of self-care rituals in promoting self-love and appreciation, we're reminded that true beauty comes from within. So go ahead, embrace your quirks, pamper yourself silly, and let your inner beauty shine brighter than a disco ball at midnight. After all, life's too short to blend in when you were born to stand out.

Chapter 5- My Façade

ToDo 1- Style Confidence Inventory

Take charge of your fashion journey by taking a deep dive into your wardrobe (not literally!) and assess your style staples. Get a clipboard, paper & pen to keep in a bathroom cabinet drawer or hang on the wall of your closet so it's always easy to grab. Start an 'inventory list' to identify pieces of clothing, makeup, hair, shoes, *panties*... that make you feel like the fierce fashionista you truly are. Each time you add to this inventory, you'll gain a deeper understanding of your style and embrace the power of self-expression.

ToDo 2- Fashion Fishbowl Week

Are you ready to shake up your style routine? Find/identify 7 accessories you like/love but do not usually wear. Cut 7 small pieces of paper and write a name for each piece down. Fold the papers and dump them all into a "fishbowl' -any bowl or big cup will do. Each day, draw one out at random and unleash your inner fashionista. Find a clever new way to design today's outfit based on your awesome accessory, then strut your stuff! Love your newfound fun, creativity, and confidence.

ToDo 3- Journal Prompt

Think back through the outfits you have felt the MOST confident in throughout your entire life: your black and white tap recital costume when you were 11, your pink-floral Senior prom dress, that new bright yellow outfit and matching hat you wore to the Kentucky Derby last May...? Write a brief description of each outfit, but write more about how it made you feel, what were your thoughts about yourself, and why were those feelings so special and memorable?

Fall In Love with: YOURSELF!

Chapter 6
My Tech

Welcome to "My Tech," where we plunge headfirst into the wild and wacky world of technology, armed with laughter, lightheartedness, and maybe just a touch of trepidation. This chapter could also be appropriately titled "The Tech Tangle: Navigating the Digital Age," as we are part of a generation that's witnessing massive change when it comes to all things tech.

From the maze of social media mishaps, digital dilemmas, and the occasional tech support session that leaves us scratching our heads in bemusement, don't forget to pat yourself on the back and give yourself some credit for being so adaptable. Yes, there may be times when you inadvertently share embarrassing selfies, or accidentally like your ex's vacation photos from three years ago. There is, of course, the hilarious side too of navigating the ever-evolving landscape of social media to explore.

As you navigate this digital jungle, bear in mind that you are not alone. Join us as we engage in side-splitting tech support sessions with younger generations, where the phrase "turn it off and on again" takes on a whole new level of comedic brilliance. From deciphering emojis to grasping the concept of a "tweetstorm," these tech support escapades guarantee to leave you in stitches. Then there are the GIFS! These are brilliant creations that are both hilarious and entertaining, but watch out, they can be addictive. For those who don't know what a GIF is, the full name of this file format is Graphics Interchange Format, to be technically accurate. GIFs are used to compress static images, primarily for online display.

And let's not overlook our online adventures—because who doesn't adore a good shopping spree or a swipe-right-worthy dating app debacle? From adding items to your cart just to reach the free shipping threshold to accidentally swiping left on your soulmate (oops), we'll delve into the humorous highs and lows of our digital escapades.

So get clicking with the mouse and scroll on as we head off on a journey through the whimsical world of "My Tech." From social media muddles and shenanigans, plus everything in between, get ready for a rollercoaster ride of laughter, mishaps, and maybe even a few "facepalm" moments along the way. After all, in the digital age, a sense of humor is the ultimate survival tool. Let's embrace the chaos with open arms (and plenty of GIFs).

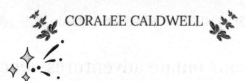

Let's Learn About It

In today's rapidly evolving online world, technology behaves like that nosy neighbor who always knows what's happening in your life. Social media platforms keep you updated on your high school crush's cat's birthday, and digital devices seem to have a mind of their own. The digital realm offers more twists and turns than a soap opera. But fear not, because even we women in our 50s can navigate this ever-changing technological maze with finesse and flair.

The ever-evolving world of technology

- Social media has been the leading catalyst in the rise of digital connections, where every like, share, and comment is a virtual high-five. These platforms shape social interactions, facilitating everything from reconnecting with long-lost friends to sharing cat memes with family members. However, controlling pesky privacy concerns and online etiquette faux pas can turn your internet paradise into a virtual nightmare. To counteract this, consider

implementing strategies such as regularly reviewing your privacy settings, being mindful of what you share publicly, and engaging authentically with your online community to create meaningful connections.

- Navigating digital spaces can sometimes feel like the Wild West of online forums and discussion groups, where opinions clash like bumper cars at rush hour. These tech spaces reshape communication patterns and social dynamics, both for better and for worse. In the digital world, it's crucial to keep your digital compass on track, as distractions and divergent online paths are easy to follow, and can make you lose focus on your original plan. You might find yourself scrolling aimlessly reading about something that was not your original intention. It's essential to grasp the significance of online literacy and safety practices, which prevent you from getting lost in the vast expanse of the internet. Here are a few tips to guide you, from the United States Attorney's Office (2015).

  - Protect your personal information: Vigilantly manage the information you share online. Refrain from disclosing sensitive personal details like your full name, address, phone number, financial details, or any data that could reveal your identity or location in the physical world. Treat personal information as currency, being selective about whom you share it with.

  - Adjust privacy settings and implement security measures: Take time to regularly check and adjust the privacy settings on your social media accounts and other online platforms to control the visibility of your posts and personal information. Create strong, unique passwords for each account and add an extra layer of security with two-factor authentication (2FA).

- Critically evaluate sources: With the internet flooded with information, discerning trustworthy sources becomes crucial. Engage in critical thinking to assess the credibility of the information you find. Seek out reputable, recognized institutions, and remain skeptical of sources lacking evidence or citations for their claims.

- Communicate respectfully: Always engage with others online respectfully, even when opinions diverge. Steer clear of conflict, seeking instead to understand varying viewpoints. Remember, real people with emotions exist behind each username and avatar.

- Recognize and report misconduct: Stay alert to signs of cyberbullying, harassment, or any online abuse. Should you or someone you know fall victim, promptly report the misconduct to platform administrators or appropriate authorities as needed.

- Be aware of your digital footprint: Exercise caution with the content you post online. Once shared on the internet, erasing something can be challenging, if not impossible. The traces you leave online can significantly impact your personal and professional life.

- Install security software: Protect your devices from malware and unauthorized access by installing and regularly updating antivirus software, firewalls, and other security tools.

- Educate yourself and others: Keep abreast of the latest online safety practices and share this knowledge with friends and family. Fostering a culture of safety and respect online paves the way for a healthier online world for all.

 • The power of accessible technology can open different doors and ways of saying hello to your old friends, and new best friends. Smartphones, tablets, and wearable technology are just a few examples of trusty companions who are here to help you stay organized, manage tasks, and access information on the go. They are like hiring a personal assistant, without the attitude. But beware of technical complexity and gadget anxiety! We all encounter common barriers when adopting new technology, but there's also plenty of assistance available to help you overcome your fear of the digital unknown.

The importance of adaptability and embracing change in a thriving tech world can be as easy as a toddler embracing a mud puddle. It's never too late to join the digital revolution!

Resistance to new technologies can hinder both personal and professional growth. Yet, it is easy to overcome such hurdles with some assistance if it is needed. Technology has many tools that inspire and offer various strategies for embracing this journey into technological change. Women in particular, who have embraced digital advancements later in life, highlight resilience and adaptability. Here are a few strategies for overcoming this resistance and getting the ball rolling, or the fingers tapping on the keyboard!

1. Education and continuous learning are some of the best ways to overcome resistance to technology. Educational workshops, online courses, and seminars can demystify new technologies and illustrate their benefits and ease of use. Community centers and libraries often hold free or low-cost training sessions designed for seniors or beginners. Participation in these programs can gradually build confidence and competence in using new digital tools.

2. Having a support network or a mentor who is proficient in technology can be incredibly beneficial. Peer groups or mentoring sessions create a safe space for asking questions and learning at a comfortable pace. Initiatives like Tech Savvy Seniors or community tech days encourage peer learning and support, often facilitated by volunteers who provide one-on-one assistance.

3. Adopting technology in small, manageable steps can reduce the feeling of being overwhelmed. Starting with the basic functions of a smartphone or computer and gradually increasing complexity can help ease the transition. Don't put undue pressure on yourself by setting your expectations too high when trying out something new for the first time. You might start by learning to send emails and gradually move on to using online banking, shopping online, or using social media platforms to connect with family and friends.

4. Connecting the use of technology to our hobbies, interests, or daily needs can greatly increase our engagement and willingness to learn. For example, learning how to make and answer a video call with your grandchildren or finding new ways to pursue your hobbies. Learning how to use apps like Skype, Zoom, or FaceTime for video chats, or introducing platforms like Pinterest for collecting ideas related to personal hobbies is a great start! These are great opportunities to engage with family members who are willing to teach you how to use these technologies.

Inspiring Stories of Women Who Embraced the Digital Age

Joan's journey from skeptic to social media savant: At 50, Joan was initially skeptical about social media. However, when her children went abroad, she decided to learn about Facebook and what benefits it offered her to stay connected. With the help of library workshops, she not only mastered Facebook but also ventured into Instagram and Twitter, becoming an avid user who now champions the benefits of staying digitally connected to her peers.

Mary's leap into e-commerce: After retiring early at 55, Mary turned her knitting hobby into a small online business. Learning to manage an online store on platforms like Etsy, she engaged with customers across the country, boosting her confidence and proving that age is just a number when it comes to entrepreneurship in the digital world.

Lindsey's literary blog: Lindsey always had a passion for writing but never pursued it seriously. At 52, she took a local course on digital literacy, which sparked the idea of starting a blog. Her blog, focusing on book reviews and literary discussions, has not only garnered a substantial following but has also rekindled her love for writing and connected her with a community of like-minded enthusiasts.

Sunita's digital photography adventure: Sunita, a 58-year-old schoolteacher, received a digital camera as a gift but was initially hesitant to use it due to her unfamiliarity with digital devices. Encouraged by her daughter, she took a beginner's course in digital photography. Now, she not only excels in capturing beautiful moments but also edits photos and shares them online, embracing her new hobby fully.

The stories of Joan, Mary, Lindsey, and Sunita showcase the transformative power of embracing new technologies, regardless of age. They demonstrate that with the right strategies—education, peer support, incremental adoption, and highlighting personal relevance—anyone can overcome resistance to technology. Their journeys inspire not only senior women but all individuals to face technological changes with curiosity and courage, ensuring they remain active, connected, and engaged in the digital age.

Lifelong learning is empowering through education and advocating this as a means of staying relevant and empowered in today's digital society is a no-brainer. Who says you can't teach an old dog new tricks? From online courses to community education programs, there's no shortage of ways to boost your digital IQ.

What They Didn't Tell Us

Setting up a new gadget often feels like wading through a labyrinth of mud without a map. To ease the pain of this process, take advantage of online tutorials and step-by-step guides offered by tech companies on their websites. YouTube channels are marvelous inventions where you have visuals and audio of how to solve your problem. You can just about YouTube anything! These useful resources can demystify the setup process and turn an otherwise frustrating and hair-pulling-out afternoon into a productive one. Never be afraid to ask for help. While you are at it, and if you are a neat freak like me, label and organize the plethora of cables that accompany all these gadgets. You will need a special "cable storage spot," which will help avoid confusion and save time in the end.

Asking younger family members or tech-savvy friends for help can be a humbling experience, and may even result in some eye-rolling, but grin and bear it, and embrace the chance to learn something new. Taking screenshots of the problems encountered, or noting down the error messages are helpful for the person helping solve the issue. It will not only help the helper

understand the issue more quickly but also teach you more about your device and its operating system. Explanations about what the problem is in as much detail as possible are also helpful other than the "it just doesn't work" statement. Clarifying the problem helps to diagnose and fix it quicker and may also even help you be able to solve the problem if it crops up again.

Tech mishaps are a comedy of errors, and we are talking about things like sending a text or email to the wrong person. Oops! This blunder is one we all have done and serves as a modern-day rite of passage into the world of tech mishaps. If this happens, and I can promise you it will, the best approach is to just fess up and admit to the mistake as quickly as you can with an explanation of the context to the unintended recipient. What's done is done, and cannot be undone. A quick, honest explanation can help lessen the embarrassment and clear up misunderstandings, hopefully swiftly.

Online shopping has taken the world by storm but it can often lead to mistakes such as ordering the wrong size or color. A week later, the mail arrives. That "one-size-fits-all" hat might fit a doll at best, and the "easy assembly required" shelf comes with instructions that seem written in an ancient cryptic language. Always make certain to double-check your cart before you check out to save time and hassle. Another good point is to also check the reviews before purchasing a product, as this can offer valuable advice. I reckon that if a person has taken the time to review a product, they have done their due diligence and are generally offering an honest review. All this will be helpful to avoid the hassle of returns and save a lot of post-online shopping stress. Remember to keep this in mind when you find yourself at midnight armed with a credit card and a dangerous level of confidence adding items to your cart with the reckless abandon of a game show contestant on a timed shopping spree.

Let's Laugh About It

In the grand tapestry of modern life, few threads prove as colorfully frustrating—and unexpectedly hilarious—as our ongoing battles with technology. For every breakthrough that promises to simplify our lives, an equal and opposite mishap awaits to test our sanity. Let's lean into the lighter side of these tech challenges, sharing a chuckle over the universal comedy that binds us all in this digital age. Let's start with a common faux pas that's become a modern classic: the misfired emoji. Similar to a text going to the wrong person but this is an emoji! Imagine you're deeply engaged in a text exchange with your boss about the latest quarterly reports, typing with business-like precision. Suddenly, amidst the barrage of texts, your thumb slips and you accidentally send a flamenco dancer instead of a thumbs up. There you are, staring at your phone, wishing you could shimmy your way out of the conversation as smoothly as your emoji just did. Instead of questioning your sudden shift toward digital dance, your boss replies with a series of equally irrelevant emojis, transforming what began as a serious business discussion into a bizarre hieroglyphic exchange. Congratulations, you've just discovered a new form of corporate communication. Our world has become so wrapped up in tech that these faux pas are becoming more the norm, even in the business world.

Then there's the evergreen ordeal of navigating automated phone menus. You know the scenario all too well: You call customer service, and the robotic voice greets you with "convenient" menu options that loop endlessly. "Press 1 for Billing," it directs, and you comply. "Press 2 for More Options," and you press again. Before you know it, you find yourself pressing numbers in a saga that leads you deeper into the automated abyss, no closer to a human voice. By the time you reach an option that vaguely relates to your original intent, you've forgotten why you called in the first place. The irony? You started this call hoping to fix your internet connection to avoid such calls in the future. Hey, it happens to all of us, so just try to see the funny in the frustration. And, remember, your call is important to them even if you have to wait for an hour or more... Let's not overlook the eternal optimism that drives us into the arms of DIY tech setup, a journey that starts with confidence and often ends with Googling phrases like, "Why is my TV speaking Spanish?" or "Help, my printer is haunted." Setting up a new gadget resembles playing a high-stakes game of technological roulette, where every step in the instruction manual is a potential pitfall. The diagram suggests cable A connects effortlessly to slot A, but in your hands, cable A seems more inclined to fit into slot Z. After several hours of struggle, you emerge victorious, your new gadget blinking to life. It doesn't matter that the living room now resembles a scene from a tech apocalypse. You've won this round. If you are going to be venturing into the world of online dating, always take a moment to review the profile of your perceived "dream date," before being tempted to swipe right and avoid awkward matchups! Most dating apps allow you to *unmatch* or block a person discreetly. Always read the fine print! Swiping right might occasionally lead to Mr. or Ms. Right, but more often, it's a cavalcade of Mr. Who's-That and Ms. How-Did-That-Happen. You might encounter a photo enthusiast who's visited every continent but can't find a date within a 10-mile radius, or the mysterious figure whose profile picture is more abstract art than portrait.

Each swipe brings a new surprise, turning your quest for love into a reality show that even the best dating advice columns couldn't prepare you for. It can provide endless hours of entertainment, even if you don't end up going on a date! In these moments, when technology feels more foe than friend, it's the shared laughter and communal groans that remind us we're all in this together. After all, what are a few misdirected emojis, hours on hold, or online shopping returns among friends? So the next time you find yourself cursing under your breath at your smartphone, remember that somewhere, someone else is doing the same thing. In the digital age, your best tool isn't the latest gadget or app—it's your sense of humor.

How to Embrace and Engage With the Changes

Adapting to, and embracing change becomes crucial, especially in this digital age. Whether we are acquiring new tech skills or staying connected through social media, finding our way through the maze of these shifts can significantly enhance both our professional and personal lives. Embracing change in the technological realm requires a proactive approach to skill acquisition and leveraging social connectivity. Not all of us will be convinced but if you haven't yet, give it a whirl! By implementing practical tips such as continuous learning, seeking guidance, and embracing trial and error, it is possible to navigate technological advancements with confidence.

Maintaining social connections through social media facilitates meaningful relationships, real-time communication, networking opportunities, and access to valuable information. Social media serves as an invaluable tool for maintaining relationships with loved ones, bridging geographical barriers, and nurturing meaningful interactions.

Here are some practical solutions and suggestions for how to overcome these often hilarious pitfalls:

- Engage in continuous learning to improve tech skills effectively. Platforms like Coursera, Udemy, and Khan Academy offer a range of courses to choose from, spanning basic computer literacy to advanced programming languages. Regular participation in these courses helps us stay updated with the latest technologies and refine our skills.

- Don't hesitate to seek guidance from tech-savvy friends, family, or colleagues. They can offer valuable insights, tips, and hands-on assistance when learning new technologies. Additionally, participating in online forums or communities related to specific tech skills facilitates knowledge-sharing and networking opportunities.

- Theory alone is insufficient; hands-on practical application is key to mastering tech skills. Challenge yourself with projects to apply acquired knowledge. Whether it's building a website, developing a mobile app, or experimenting with data analysis, practice reinforces understanding and boosts confidence.

- Embrace trial and error when it comes to tech skills. Rather than fearing mistakes, consider them as learning opportunities. Each error provides insights into potential solutions and enhances problem-solving abilities.

- Utilize features like instant messaging and video calling offered by platforms such as WhatsApp, Facebook Messenger, and Skype for real-time communication regardless of distance. These tools create spontaneous conversations and connections with each other, enabling us to share life moments as if we were together in person.

- We can gain access to information and take steps to empower ourselves through the knowledge available through the internet. Technology provides access to information and resources on everything from health and finance to education and personal development. But beware of misinformation! The importance of digital literacy and critical thinking skills cannot be emphasized enough to ensure we can separate fact from fiction in the digital age.

- We can amplify our voices and advocate for change, especially when it involves making some noise about social, political, or economic issues. A digital voice is loud! From online activism to digital storytelling, technology gives us the tools to create real-world impact from the comfort of our own homes. Think about all the amazing causes you could lend your voice to over anywhere in the world because of the internet!

As we reflect on technology's profound impact on our world, one thing becomes clear: Adaptability and embracing technology are essential for staying connected, informed, and empowered in today's digital age. So let's embrace change, prioritize lifelong learning, and harness the power of technology to shape a brighter future for ourselves and generations to come. After all, in the digital age, the only limit is your imagination. Let's make it a journey to remember!

Chapter 6- My Tech

ToDo 1- Online Learning Course

There are SO many places online to learn from. Today or tomorrow, sit down and browse through a couple "platforms" that have courses that interest you. ("Platforms" is just a fancy word for the name of the website that holds/hosts several choices of classes. The BIG names are Coursera.com, Thinkific.com, Udemy.com, and Teachable.com, but there are tons more!) Search things like: online card making course, online Spanish course, online virtual Holy Land tour, etc... Literally, whatever you have an interest in, there IS a course for it online. Learn something, make something, plan something, experience something; you can do it all from your comfy couch! What will you sign up for?

Enroll in one course:_____

Platform:_____

Engage, Embrace, Empower: YOU!

ToDo 2- Virtual Networking

Organize a virtual networking "reunion-call" with 2 or more friends, past or present: best friends, old college friends, all your bridesmaids, book club girls, etc... This is going to teach you new tech skills while opening up a whole new world of communication possibilities!

1. Choose a date and time that will be convenient for most of your girlfriends to attend (log-on).
2. Hopefully, you've at least heard of Zoom, Google Meet, Microsoft Teams, GoTo Meeting or Skype. Choose one of these platforms, create a login profile, then follow the steps it gives to plan a future meeting. It will provide you with a meeting ID number & passcode, and a strange-looking invite link (ie: https://us04web.zoom.us/j/72908...).
3. There will be a way for you to share this invitation link with your friends. Click on it, then send it to them in a text or an email.
4. Log on 10 minutes before your "reunion call" so you can get comfortable and situated. You are the HOST, so you are the one who clicks the button to 'begin' the meeting and allows participants (your friends) to join. Make sure to start your meeting on time.
5. Just have fun talking to your friends. Because you are the host, this call isn't the one for you to start experimenting with backgrounds and other fun/silly/crazy options. Save this for your next calls so you don't accidentally 'hang-up' on everyone! Believe me, I've done it...
6. When you are done, don't forget to log off/sign-out.

Congratulations, you've done it!. You've Hosted your first live video conference. Hope it was something you feel you could do again, because it is a tremendous way to keep in touch with out-of-town family or friends, and also a way just to bring people in different places together as a team.

Engage, Embrace, Empower: YOU!

ToDo 3– Tech Problem reflection

Describe a recent experience where you encountered a technological challenge or problme. How did you adapt and approach solving it?

_____

_____

_____

_____

_____

_____

_____

_____

_____

_____

_____

_____

_____

_____

_____

_____

_____

_____

_____

_____

Falling in Love with Your Tech

There is no escaping that tech is very much a part of our daily lives, offering countless opportunities for connection, productivity, and enjoyment. While some may feel intimidated by the rapid pace of technological advancements, embracing technology with confidence and a sense of humor can lead to a fulfilling and enriching experience. Let's explore some stories of women who have embraced technology in their 50s and have found joy and empowerment in integrating it into their lives. Remember, embracing technology at any age is possible!

These two stories are about empowerment and keeping the connection with family strong.

- Sarah is a vibrant woman in her 50s who initially felt overwhelmed by the complexities of technology. However, with determination and curiosity, Sarah decided to "grab the mouse" and head off on a journey to become tech-savvy. She discovered the power of video calls to connect with her grandchildren who lived across the country. Through regular virtual chats, Sarah strengthened her bond with her family and witnessed her grandchildren grow and flourish despite the distance.

- Then there's Samantha, who, after retiring, found herself with newfound time and a desire to explore her passions. She immersed herself in the world of online communities and discovered a vibrant community of fellow gardening enthusiasts. Through online forums and social media groups, she exchanged tips, advice, and stories with like-minded individuals, enriching her gardening experience and forming lasting friendships along the way. She even started writing her book, or rather, typing it onto a Word document!

Find joy in digital tools that simplify daily tasks and offer unparalleled convenience. After all, who doesn't like some extra free time to do whatever suits your fancy? The ease of task improvements they offer range from meal planning apps that streamline grocery shopping lists, to smart home devices that automate your lights and household chores! Technology has revolutionized the way we live our lives.

• Jane embraced the convenience of meal delivery services after busy workdays. With a few taps on her smartphone, she could order fresh, healthy meals tailored to her dietary preferences, saving her time and energy without compromising on quality. It all took very little effort, and she found choosing meals a lot of fun.

 • Sue found solace in meditation and mindfulness apps that helped her manage stress and prioritize self-care. With guided meditation sessions and relaxation exercises available at her fingertips, she could carve out moments of tranquility amidst her hectic schedule, leading to a greater sense of balance and well-being.

Cultivating a growth mindset goes hand-in-hand with using technology with confidence. It requires a sense of curiosity and willingness to learn. Rather than feel intimidated by unfamiliar gadgets or software (that's the program inside the computer), approaching them with an open mind and a sense of adventure is a far better option. It's okay to make mistakes along the way, but remember to celebrate your successes, no matter how small they may seem. I remember the victory I felt when I realized the inner X of the window that I had opened wouldn't close the outer window to the program itself. Sounds so simple, now but boy, was it a great moment then. It took me a while to admit that seemingly really silly thing, as I felt it was a bit stupid to not just know it. Don't let your insecurities cloud a funny moment like I did.

So, whether you're video chatting with loved ones, exploring new hobbies online, or simplifying your daily tasks with digital tools, remember that the world of technology is yours to explore and enjoy. Embrace it with open arms, and you'll discover endless possibilities for growth, connection, empowerment, and humor.

Fall In Love with: YOURSELF!

Chapter- 6 My Tech

ToDo 1- Tech skill challenge:

[This challenge may sound a bit ambiguous because it has to be personalized for your own needs.]

Set a specific, tech-related skill to improve on or learn this week/month.

- Learn how to code at Codecademy
- Master how to type a letter in Microsoft Word
- Create to-do or packing lists using a spreadsheet template
- Edit photos or videos with Adobe Creative Suite
- Experiment with the basics of graphic design using Procreate or Canva
- Record and edit your recording on Audacity or GarageBand

While it is impossible to list everything, these examples provide some guidance. The aim is to strengthen your proficiency and confidence through effort and practice. Feel free to learn as long and as much as you can, but set a specific, time-based goal so you have a way to measure your achievement.

"In _____days, I will...

-be able to-   or   -know how to-   or   -understand the basics

of-_____ because of my

daily efforts and practice using _____."

 # Fall In Love with: YOURSELF!

ToDo 2- Digital Detox Day

This is an essential component when it comes to living in this sometimes overwhelming digital age. It entails disconnecting from all electronic devices and digital platforms for a designated period. Going screen-free encourages the promotion of well-being, and emphasizes the importance of face-to-face interactions, spending time in nature, or practicing hobbies and activities that do not necessitate technology.   Just so there's no cheating, this means...

NO Smartphones

NO Computers- everything on them!

NO Social media: Facebook, Instagram, Twitter, TikTok, etc.

NO Video or TV streaming

NO Gaming

NO. Email: unless it's necessary for work or urgent matters.

NO Internet

NO Digital entertainment: audiobooks, digital music, etc.

NO Digital communication

NO Online shopping

NO TV and/or News shows

You **CAN**- listen to AM/FM radio stations, talk on a land-line phone (if you still have one), read the printed newspaper and books, put together a puzzle, play with grandchildren, go fishing (no gps-fishfinders!), bake your famous cookies, etc.

Fall In Love with: YOURSELF!

ToDo 3– Livin' In A Tech Revolution!

So much has and is changing! We have all fallen in love with technology somehow in our lives. Reflect on how transformative technology has been in your life. Describe how it has enriched your daily experiences, empowered you to pursue your passions, or strengthened your connections with others. In what ways has technology changed your perspective on the world or people around you?

_____

_____

_____

_____

_____

_____

_____

_____

_____

_____

_____

_____

_____

_____

_____

_____

_____

_____

_____

_____

Fall In Love with: YOURSELF!

Chapter 7
My Time

As we climb up and down the proverbial peaks and valleys of our professional lives, it's crucial to carve out time for hobbies and passions outside of work. Otherwise, you may find yourself at a bit of a loss when the time comes to retire. However, what starts as a sincere endeavor to cultivate a new skill or pursue a lifelong dream can quickly morph into a comedy of errors. But, it doesn't matter, does it?

Striking a balance between work and pleasure takes center stage. As we juggle professional commitments, family obligations, and personal passions, finding harmony in our lives becomes a constant challenge—and a source of endless laughter. From scheduling lists to unexpected curveballs, mastering the art of balance and imbalance is a journey filled with chuckles, lessons, and the occasional well-deserved siesta.

Passion projects have a knack for exposing our hidden talents—or lack thereof—in the most unexpected ways. Whether it's attempting to master a musical instrument, perfecting the art of gourmet cooking, or tackling DIY home renovations, the journey from novice to expert is riddled with laughter, mishaps, and the occasional charred soufflé.

This decade isn't merely about aging gracefully; it's about embracing the comedic chaos that comes with it. As we step into this new chapter of life, we're met with a whirlwind of adventures, challenges, and unexpected moments of hilarity.

Ah, the notorious "J" word—job. It serves as the cornerstone of our adult lives, where we dedicate the lion's share of our waking hours. And let's be honest, it's a fertile ground for comedic gold regarding scaling the comedic career ladder. From office antics to corporate blunders, navigating the workplace in our 50s presents an array of hurdles and moments that make us burst into laughter. We care less about the stuff that truly doesn't matter.

I never imagined I'd encounter the proverbial glass ceiling when I was at the peak of my career. Yet, amidst the absurdity of office politics and the relentless chase for that elusive corner office, I often found humor. Who needs a corner office when you can enjoy a front-row seat to the daily comedy show that is corporate life?

Making a triumphant exit from the workforce is a goal many of us aspire to as we approach retirement. Whether it's retiring to a beachside haven or pursuing a passion project, bidding adieu to the nine-to-five grind can be both liberating and downright hysterical. For some, it even means continuing to work, but in a different environment.

Carving out time for travel and leisure is a top priority for many of us in our 50s, but it wouldn't be a genuine adventure without a healthy dose of humor thrown into the mix. It probably should be called globetrotting giggles rather than travel and leisure. From lost luggage to language barriers, navigating the world of travel in our 50s is a comedy waiting to unfold, if you let it. Whether it's getting lost in translation or inadvertently boarding the wrong flight, every misadventure becomes a cherished memory and a side-splitting story to share with friends and family back home.

Who says you have to venture far and wide to have a blast? Staycations offer the perfect opportunity to explore our backyards and indulge in some much-needed relaxation without straying too far from home. Whether it's binge-watching our favorite TV show, tackling a DIY home improvement project, or simply lounging by the pool with a good book, finding joy at home is an art form in itself.

From career calamities to hobby hijinks, this decade should be loaded with humor, heart, and a healthy dose of laughter along the way to prepare us for the decades ahead. After all, isn't laughter the best medicine for life's twists and turns?

Let's Learn About It

No matter how old you are, life's journey is a constant flux of challenges and opportunities, each stage presenting its unique blend of trials and triumphs. In our contemporary society, the dynamics of time management, career pursuits, and leisure engagements have undergone significant transformations.

How do we explore the distinct challenges and opportunities encountered during our 50s? The emphasis should be placed on the importance of maximizing our time, both in our professional endeavors and personal pursuits.

Challenges and opportunities in time management

- Effective time management emerges as a critical element during this life stage, where the intricate balance between work, family, and personal commitments looms large. Negotiating this equilibrium can appear daunting, as it is common to experience moments that crop up and you can find yourself grappling with the demands of a thriving career alongside the pursuit of leisure and fulfillment.

• The sensation of time scarcity stands out as a predominant challenge during this phase. As responsibilities accumulate, a feeling of being overwhelmed and stretched thin is quite normal. This heightened pressure can precipitate escalated stress levels and a pervasive sense of dissatisfaction with the allocation of time (Segal et al., 2023). More importantly, as we mature, the realization of time's finite nature becomes increasingly palpable, intensifying the urgency of living life to its fullest.

However, amidst these hurdles, lies a wealth of opportunities for personal growth and fulfillment. Proficient time management skills can bolster productivity, cultivate a harmonious work-life balance, and augment overall well-being. By defining priorities, setting pragmatic goals, and employing efficiency-enhancing strategies, time can be harnessed more effectively, realizing objectives with greater efficiency as you find out what time management strategies work for you.

Furthermore, this life stage often heralds a period of introspection and reevaluation, prompting you to scrutinize your values and aspirations. Embracing these contemplative junctures can pave the way for newfound avenues of personal and professional development, culminating in a more gratifying and purpose-driven existence.

Managing careers

Balancing ambition and practicality is important when managing your career in your 50s. Many find themselves at a crossroads, grappling with the tension between career aspirations and familial or personal commitments.

- For many in their 50s, one big hurdle is feeling the pressure to hit major career goals by certain deadlines. Whether it's climbing the corporate ladder, starting a new business, or trying out fresh career paths, there's often this rush to make big professional leaps. And when those targets are not met, it can mess with your mojo, leaving you feeling a sense of inadequacy or self-doubt.

However, let's not forget that finding career happiness goes beyond just the paycheck and that fancy job title. Somehow reaching your 50s brings along a sense of wanting to find joy and meaning in work that truly speaks to the soul, even if it means ditching those traditional markers of success. Embracing this shift in mindset can lead to a genuine and fulfilling career journey before it is too late.

This life stage opens up opportunities for career metamorphosis and exploration. Armed with years of experiential wisdom, allow yourself to feel emboldened to venture into uncharted territories, whether through entrepreneurial pursuits, passion projects, or sectoral transitions. This phase thus emerges as a fertile ground for professional renaissance and reinvention.

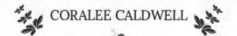
Making the most of leisure activities

While career pursuits are pivotal, the pursuit of leisure activities assumes equal significance in fostering holistic well-being and fulfillment. However, amidst the whirlwind of professional and personal responsibilities, carving out time for leisure pursuits can prove to be a formidable challenge. It is imperative to underscore the indispensability of leisure to nurture the balance of emotional health and avoid any chance of burnout.

- Overcoming the guilt associated with indulging in leisure activities is something you are certainly not alone in. We live in a culture that pushes productivity and busyness, and there often exists an inclination to prioritize work over leisure, so that personal interests and hobbies get relegated to the sidelines. Over time, this behavior can precipitate heightened stress levels and a diminished sense of life satisfaction.

Leisure pursuits are for more than just to experience relaxation; they constitute a pathway for personal growth and enrichment. Hobbies allow avenues for self-expression, creativity, and exploration. Whether it entails delving into artistic pursuits, partaking in sporting events, or immersing oneself in nature's splendor, leisure activities bring a wellspring of joy and gratification. They also serve as catalysts for fortifying social bonds and building a better sense of community. Whether through club memberships, social gatherings, or altruistic endeavors, leisure pursuits provide fertile grounds for connections with kindred spirits, thereby mitigating feelings of isolation and nurturing emotional resilience.

Managing time effectively, steering professional goals, and reveling in leisure pursuits during this life stage present a multifaceted tapestry of challenges and opportunities. Acknowledging the cardinal importance of optimizing our time allocation, both in our vocational and personal spheres results in traversing this time with enhanced resilience and gratification. By seizing upon avenues for growth, reinvention, and leisure, life is more balanced with meaning, purpose, and boundless fulfillment.

What They Didn't Tell Us

This is where we include the unspoken truths about work, retirement, and pursuing passions: It can be a bit of a roller coaster but with that, there's never a dull moment either!

Workplace warfare: Where experience battles buzzwords

Ah, the joys of the modern office. Many people never join the corporate world, but we've all seen it in movies or on TV. Navigating the ever-shifting landscape of corporate culture, where experience battles the latest buzzwords and team-building exercises leave you questioning your sanity. Let's face it, turning 50 doesn't magically shield you from these mishaps. Sometimes it throws a whole new set of curveballs. Suddenly, you find yourself surrounded by colleagues who could be your children (and sometimes act like them too). Their preferred communication method? Memes and emojis. Their solution to every problem? A brainstorming session fueled by kombucha and free snacks (because apparently, sugar crashes lead to brilliant ideas).

War story Wednesday: The case of the disappearing deadlines

Remember that crucial report due next week? You've meticulously researched, crafted compelling arguments, and formatted the whole thing with color-coded charts. You proudly present it to your team, only to be met with blank stares and a chorus of "What's a pivot table?" Turns out, your young colleague tasked with uploading the data interpreted "pivot table" as a literal suggestion to physically rotate the desks for "better creative flow." Needless to say, the deadline danced off into the ether. But hey, here's the upside: Your experience is a goldmine. You've seen trends come and go, deciphered cryptic management speak, and navigated office politics with the grace of a seasoned diplomat. Remember that presentation you delivered while sleep-deprived from a toddler's teething phase? Or the time you single-handedly saved the client when the server crashed (and all you needed was a good old-fashioned restart, not a team of tech wizards armed with laptops)? Yeah, you've got this.

The glass ceiling: It's cracked, not shattered

You've all heard the term "glass ceiling," that invisible barrier supposedly holding women back in their careers. But what if it's not a ceiling at all? Maybe it's a warped window offering a distorted view. Perhaps your version of success doesn't involve a corner office and a team of assistants fetching your triple-shot lattes. Maybe it's about flexible hours, remote work, or pursuing a passion project alongside your day job.

Let's take a moment to celebrate women who redefined success on their terms. Look at Iris Apfel, a fashion icon who hit her stride in her 80s (Wikipedia, 2020). Or Julia Child, who revolutionized American cuisine at the ripe old age of 50 (Wikipedia, 2019). Age is just a number, and your definition of success is yours to craft.

The power of "No"

Don't be afraid to say no to opportunities that don't align with your goals. Just because your ambitious boss thinks a 70-hour work week is the key to success doesn't mean you have to subscribe to that philosophy. It's okay to prioritize your well-being and carve out time for yourself and your passions.

Retirement: The big maybe (and sometimes maybe not)

Retirement. The word conjures images of piña coladas on pristine beaches. But for many women, the reality is far less glamorous. Social Security checks might not stretch as far as we'd hoped, and the thought of leaving behind the structure and identity work provides can be daunting.

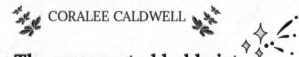

Oops, I didn't plan for this: The unexpected hobbyist

My neighbor, a brilliant engineer, retired at 65 with grand plans for volunteering work and travel. Turns out, the bureaucracy of volunteer organizations and the jet lag of international travel weren't quite the adventure she envisioned. After a year of feeling lost, she stumbled upon a local beekeeping class. Now, she's managing a thriving hive in her backyard, supplying her community with delicious honey, and has a newfound appreciation for the buzzing world of bees. Retirement doesn't have to be a one-size-fits-all proposition. It can be a chance to explore new passions, volunteer your skills, or simply relax and recharge.

Let's Laugh About It

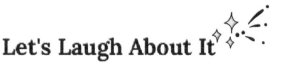

Bloopers transform into bonding experiences, particularly in the context of the ever-evolving work landscape and the drive to uncover hidden talents through new hobbies. Here's a chance to celebrate the lighter side of these experiences, proving that we're all in this together. We might trip over metaphorical banana peels, but hey, at least we emerge with a good story, and maybe a slightly bruised ego.

From boardroom to balance beam battles: Team building gone wild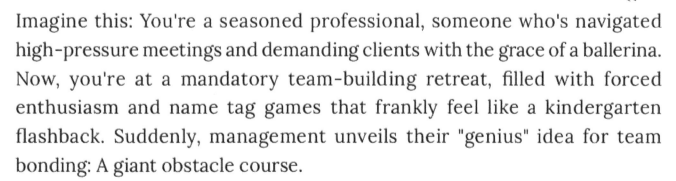

Imagine this: You're a seasoned professional, someone who's navigated high-pressure meetings and demanding clients with the grace of a ballerina. Now, you're at a mandatory team-building retreat, filled with forced enthusiasm and name tag games that frankly feel like a kindergarten flashback. Suddenly, management unveils their "genius" idea for team bonding: A giant obstacle course.

Fast forward ten minutes. You, along with your colleagues, a delightful mix of millennials and Gen Zers, are staring down a towering wall, a wobbly balance beam, and a pit of what suspiciously resembles... green Jell-O. This is your chance to shine, right? Wrong. Your 50-year-old knees decide they've had enough of this playground torture. As you attempt to scale the wall with the agility of a sloth, your grip fails, and you find yourself face-planting into the green Jell-O with a resounding "splat."

The initial shock gives way to a wave of laughter, both from yourself and your team. Turns out, even the most stoic coworker enjoys a good belly laugh, especially when it involves someone (you) covered in Jell-O. The takeaway? Maybe leave the obstacle courses to the younger crowd and stick to impressing everyone with your negotiation skills back in the office.

Seeking Zen through kayaking: My journey to becoming one with the river (and the catfish)

Remember that childhood dream of conquering the rapids in a sleek kayak? Turns out, that dream translates a little differently in your 50s. Fueled by a desire for adventure, and a slight midlife crisis, you sign up for a kayaking class. The brochure promised serenity on the water, a chance to reconnect with nature. What they didn't mention was the possibility of becoming a catfish's midday snack.

The first lesson starts smoothly. Well, as smoothly as paddling a wobbly boat can be. You're surrounded by fellow enthusiasts, a mix of ages and experience levels. But then, disaster strikes. A rogue wave or a particularly enthusiastic catfish decides to test your newfound kayaking skills. The kayak tips violently, and before you can react, you find yourself in the chilly embrace of the river, face-to-face with one very surprised catfish.

Soaked but surprisingly uninjured, except for your pride, you haul yourself back into the kayak, vowing not to give up. The rest of the lesson is a hilarious exercise in regaining balance and avoiding further catfish encounters. By the end, you've conquered the basics of paddling (mostly) in a straight line and emerged with a newfound respect for the power of water and the audacity of catfish.

The point? Learning a new skill at this stage in life is all about embracing the journey. Laugh at the mishaps, celebrate the small victories, and don't be afraid to develop a healthy respect for catfish.

Master chef or master of disaster?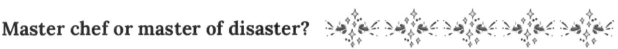

Inspired by those mouthwatering cooking shows, you decide to unleash your inner Gordon Ramsay (minus the yelling, and the swearing, perhaps, or not!). Armed with a fancy new cookbook and a cart full of exotic ingredients, (because who doesn't love a side dish of star anise?) you embark on your culinary adventure.

Except, your kitchen quickly resembles a war zone. The food processor groans in protest as you attempt to pulverize almonds into fine dust... cue smoke alarm! The delicately crafted saffron risotto turns a suspicious shade of gray, and the "simple" French pastry recipe leaves you questioning the meanings of "simple" and "pastry."

But amidst the kitchen chaos, there are moments of triumph. You manage to salvage the risotto with a generous helping of parmesan cheese because cheese fixes everything, right? The "rustic" look of your pastry becomes a conversation starter at your next dinner party. And most importantly, you learn a valuable lesson–cooking shows make everything look way easier than it is.

The beauty of venturing into a new hobby, especially cooking, is that even disasters can be delicious, or at least edible. It's about experimenting and having some fun.

How to Engage and Embrace the Changes

Your 50s are meant to be a time of flourishing careers, and supportive families (hopefully!). It could even be a time when a burning desire to finally learn how to play the ukulele pops up, but more on that later. But let's face it, all this "living your best life" comes with new challenges and new strategies.

Juggling work deadlines, family commitments, and the pursuit of your newfound passions can feel like wrestling a particularly energetic tiger. Don't worry, fellow warriors, there are ways to tame this time beast and emerge victorious, and maybe even with a few ukulele tunes under your belt!

Here are some practical strategies specifically designed for the dynamic lives of women in their 50s

- Feeling overwhelmed by a never-ending to-do list? Batch similar tasks together. Dedicate specific times for emails, phone calls, errands, or even creative pursuits. This helps you stay focused and avoid the mental drain of context-switching. Imagine the satisfaction of crossing off a whole batch of tasks at once–a productivity power move if I've ever seen one. Hey, I have even written a list of what I have achieved and then immediately ticked it off for some self-satisfaction!

- We live in a golden age of time-saving apps and digital tools. Utilize calendar apps to schedule appointments, grocery delivery services to free up weekend time, and online learning platforms to explore new hobbies. The key is to be mindful—technology should be your ally, not your master.

- Don't be a control freak! Delegate tasks at work and home. Empower your colleagues, and enlist the help of your family—even teenagers can be surprisingly useful creatures! And don't be afraid to outsource chores... hello, cleaning services!

- Schedule "me time," and stick to it. Treat "me time" like you would any other important appointment. Block out time in your calendar for activities that bring you joy, whether it's reading a book, taking a relaxing bath, or finally conquering that ukulele.

- Boundaries might sound like a fancy psychological term, but in reality, they're the invisible fences that protect your precious time and sanity. They are the secret weapon of the time-crunched woman. Setting clear boundaries between work and leisure is crucial for maintaining a healthy balance in your 50s. Here's how to do it like a pro:

  ○ Communicate clearly: Talk to your boss, colleagues, and family about your desired boundaries. Explain your need for dedicated work hours and uninterrupted personal time.

- Silence the after-hours siren song: Resist the urge to check work emails or respond to calls outside of your designated work hours. This sends a clear message that you value your time and deserve a break.

- The art of saying goodbye without guilt. It's okay to leave work at work. Don't feel obligated to attend every after-work event or social gathering. Prioritize your energy and choose activities that truly nourish you.

Success stories: Women who mastered the balance

Let's face it, sometimes the best inspiration comes from seeing others walk the walk. Here are two examples of famous women who have mastered the art of juggling career, family, and personal pursuits in their 50s and beyond:

Michelle Obama: Former First Lady, bestselling author, and mother of two, Michelle Obama is a shining example of balancing a demanding public life with personal fulfillment. Her dedication to family time and her advocacy for healthy living demonstrate the importance of prioritizing both work and personal well-being.

Oprah Winfrey: Media mogul, philanthropist, and talk show icon, Oprah Winfrey built an empire while maintaining a strong sense of self and a commitment to helping others. She is a testament to the power of finding your passion and pursuing it no matter your background, with unwavering dedication, while also nurturing personal connections.

You don't need to be famous to enjoy success—these two women just serve as reminders of women who have succeeded when they had many challenges ahead of them, despite their wealth and fame. Remember, you are not alone in this juggling act! Every woman's journey is unique, and the key to success lies in persevering in whatever goals you have set for yourself.

Chapter 7- My Time

ToDo 1- Time Audit

This activity allows for a clearer picture to be gained of how you currently spend your time. Divide a piece of paper (or a Word doc) into four sections titled: Work, family/friends, "Me Time", and sleep.

Work	Family/Friends	"Me Time"	Sleep

Track each of these activities for a full week and be honest! Include everything from work and personal calls, scrolling through social media, binge-watching Netflix, preparing meals, walking the dog/exercise, to staring out the window.

Analyze your information at the end of the week by either counting specific hours or just making general percentages of how your time was spent.

This past week, how many hour or whay percentage of time did I spend on:

Work	Family/Friends	"Me Time"	Sleep
_____	_____	_____	_____

Engage, Embrace, Empower: YOU!

ToDo 2- Master Schedule Revamp

Whatever "planner" system you use now may be working just fine, but it's FUN and new insights may be gained by trying something different. Pick a NEW scheduling tool, whichever type works for you- online calendars/planners or paper & pen designs. Try using it for two weeks. Add colors, symbols, and emojis for different categories. If you're using actual paper, use colored pens, washi tape, & stickers to make it more fun! A visual layout will help you slot in hours for your various commitments, conquer all those to-do lists, and ensure that you still leave time for that ever-so-important "me time."

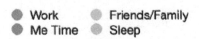

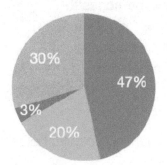

(Example pie chart)

ToDo 3- A Reflection of My Time

Use this circle to create a pie chart of your time audit from ToDo 1.

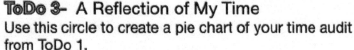

Engage, Embrace, Empower: YOU!

ToDo 3- ...continued

A. What surprised you the most about your time audit findings?

B. What are 3 ways that you can manage your time more effectively so you can schedule at least one "me time" activities into every day?

A.

B.

Engage, Embrace, Empower: YOU!

Falling in Love With Your Time

Your 50s. A time often associated with slowing down, maybe rocking a comfortable pair of yoga pants more frequently, because who needs jeans that don't have an elastic waistband anymore? *Whaaaaaaaaaaaaaaat??* Only kidding!!

Instead of viewing this decade as the end of something, let's celebrate it as the beginning of a whole new chapter—one filled with the freedom to truly fall in love with *your* time.

This means embracing both your career and your personal life with renewed passion. It's about rediscovering what sets your soul on fire, whether it's climbing the corporate ladder with the tenacity of a champion rock climber or mastering the art of macramé, because hey, fringe is back in style!

Gone are the days when your career path was a straight line leading to retirement. Today, women who are in their 50s are rewriting the script of success. Take Samantha, for instance, a former corporate accountant who followed her lifelong dream of opening a bakery. Now, surrounded by the sweet aroma of freshly baked bread, she embodies the fulfillment that comes from pursuing a passion project.

Or consider Jennifer who left her high-pressure law firm to become a yoga instructor. Trading the boardroom for a serene yoga studio, she found peace and purpose she never experienced in the legal world. Her story shows the importance of listening to your inner voice and making changes that align with your values.

These are just two examples of countless women who have ventured onto exciting new paths in their 50s. Their journeys inspire us to re-evaluate our definitions of success and embrace the possibilities ahead. Maybe it's time to dust off that business plan for your handcrafted jewelry line or finally sign up for that pottery class you've been eyeing for years. Who knows? Your 50s might just be the decade you reinvent yourself and discover your true calling.

The symphony of self-expression: Hobbies as a gateway to fulfillment

Remember when coloring was just for kids? Well, guess what? Adult coloring books are a thing, a glorious and surprisingly therapeutic thing. This explosion of creativity in hobbies highlights shows that pursuing your passions isn't just about fun; it's about self-expression and self-care.

Whether it's painting landscapes, learning to play a ukulele (yes, that again) serenading your slightly bewildered pets, or mastering the art of knitting luxurious scarves, hobbies offer a way to express yourself outside of the daily grind. There's a sense of accomplishment that comes from mastering a new skill, a quiet joy as you lose yourself in the creative process. I thought I was a natural at pottery, only to end up with a lopsided creation that resembled a misshapen mushroom more than a vase. I just laughed it off and shared the picture with my friends, who also found it funny but were there for support, love, and laughter. I will try again as pottery is a passion, but this time with renewed determination and maybe a little more practice.

Indulging in these pastimes can be a powerful stress reliever, offering a much-needed escape from the pressures of work and life. Yes, there may be moments of frustration like struggling with a wayward knitting needle or trying to decipher cryptic DIY instructions, but that's all part of the journey. You might even use some of that newfound tech knowledge from the last chapter to look up directions on YouTube!

Approach your hobbies with a lighthearted spirit. Don't be afraid to experiment, make mistakes, and laugh at yourself along the way. After all, the journey toward mastery is half the fun!

Falling in love with your time isn't a one-time event; it's a continuous adventure. Constantly seek new ways to engage your mind, nurture your spirit, and find joy in everything you do. Remember, it's never too late to explore new interests, rekindle old passions, and inject a healthy dose of humor into your life. So, go forth, rewrite that to-do list with activities you truly enjoy, and fall madly headfirst into this awesome chapter of life!

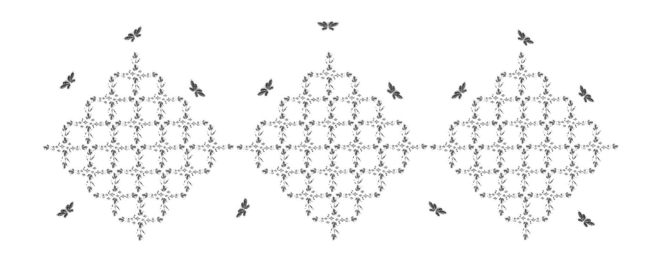

Chapter 7- My Time

ToDo 1- Time-Blocking Challenge

This is similar to the time audit but this technique involves dedicating specific blocks of time in your day for focused work on particular tasks. Here's how to conquer the challenge:

1. Make a list of all the tasks you need to accomplish this week.
2. Group them all into categories: work, home, ME, etc... for maximum efficiency. Assign each Group a color. (Tiny, colored dot-stickers, markers, washi tape, computer text colors or background highlights, etc...)
3. Choose whatever planner you love using the most.
4. Block out (using your colors) specific time slots in your calendar for each task category.
5. Unexpected events arise? They will, don't panic! See where you can fit them in and adjust your schedule as needed.

Just try your best to stick to your designated time blocks this week so you can truly focus on productivity and effective use of your time.

Fall In Love with: YOURSELF!

ToDo 2- 10 Minutes of Passion

Ever feel like your life is stuck on autopilot? This list is your ticket to rediscovering what ignites your soul. Here's how to unlock your inner passion:

10 min

Take 10 "Me-Time" minutes to brainstorming activities that have always piqued your interest. Did you dream of becoming a painter as a child? Maybe you secretly harbor a desire to learn how to play the banjo. Jot down EVERYTHING that comes to mind, no matter how outlandish it may seem. Use brainstorming bubbles or a bulleted list — anything that inspires you to write.

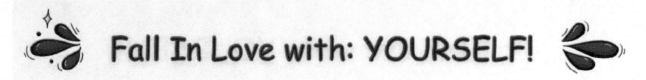

Fall In Love with: YOURSELF!

ToDo 3- Comedy at work (without getting fired!)

Let's be honest, work isn't *always* humorless. Injecting a healthy dose of humor into your workday can boost morale, strengthen relationships with colleagues, and even improve productivity. Here are some ways to lighten the mood without getting a stern talking-to from your boss. Try some out; maybe even enlist a co-worker's help.

- Find a hilarious meme that perfectly captures the struggle of that never-ending spreadsheet. Share it with your colleagues, assuming workplace policies allow it.
- Did your team finally crack a challenging project? Celebrate with a funny anecdote or a playful round of high-fives.
- Place funny sayings or quotes inside bathroom stalls.
- Play the 2-Truths-1-Lie game at a catered lunch or a meeting
- Pass out a photocopy of paper airplane instructions
- Celebrate the crazy holidays like, Strawberry Ice Cream Day 1/15, Pi Day 3/14, Dog Appreciation Day 8/26, or "Talk like a Pirate Day 9/19
- Pin up <u>complimentary</u> pics of co-workers 'photoshopped' as Super Heroes
- Pass out gummy bears or some other kids' treat at a meeting
- Create wall space to display "Look at what my kid made!" for all to contribute masterpieces of school artwork made by their children/nieces/nephews/grandkids, random-liked-kids...
- Institute Monday Moves from 12:00-12:04- Host a Dance Off, Dance Line, or just Dance Time! You could even have weekly themes and a roving trophy prize.

What kind of humor resonates with your colleagues? Remember, the goal here is to create a positive and productive atmosphere, not get written up for inappropriate behavior. Focus on lighthearted observations or witty banter. Avoid offensive jokes, and steer clear of anything considered unprofessional controversial, political or unaligned with your work policies and guidelines.   Get prior approval whenever necessary!

Fall In Love with: YOURSELF!

ToDo 4- Brainstorming Pursuits

Pick the 2 potential pursuits you're most interested in from ToDo 2's 10 Minutes of Passion, and answer these 3 questions.

1. What excites you about this activity?
2. How would pursuing this hobby enrich your life?
3. Is there a specific course you can take, a workshop, or a club you can join? Take action!

1st pursuit-

_____

_____

_____

_____

_____

_____

_____

_____

2nd pursuit-

_____

_____

_____

_____

_____

_____

_____

_____

Chapter 8
My Family Roles

How many of these ROLES have you played sometime in the last 30 years?
(Check the boxes as you go)

☐ A Nurturer/Caretaker -She provides emotional support, care, and nurturing to other family members. -She takes responsibility for the well-being and needs of family members.	☐ A Homemaker -She manages household tasks, such as cooking, cleaning, and organizing. -She creates a comfortable and nurturing home environment.
☐ A Provider -She ensures the family's financial stability by contributing to income which provides, at the least, for the basic needs of everyone. -She manages financial responsibilities and budget plans.	☐ A Caregiver -She provides physical care and assistance, especially in times of illness or need. -She takes responsibility for the health and well-being of family members .
☐ A Leader/Decision-Maker -She takes on a leadership role in making decisions for the family. -She guides and influences family choices and direction.	☐ A Problem-Solver -She approaches challenges with a solution-based mindset. -She collaborates with family members to address issues.
☐ A Peacemaker/Mediator -She helps resolve conflicts, models, and teaches positive communication. -She works to prevent discord and maintain unity within the family.	☐ A Friend/Companion -She builds and maintains close relationships within the family. -She offers companionship, loyalty, and a sense of belonging.
☐ A Educator/Mentor -She guides and supports the educational and personal development of family members. -She shares knowledge, values, and life skills.	☐ A Supporter/Encourager -She offers encouragement and positive reinforcement. -She provides emotional support during challenges or transitions.
☐ A Role Model -She sets a positive example through behavior, values, and ethical standards. -She inspires other family members to emulate positive traits.	☐ A Listener/Communicator -She listens actively to family members' concerns, ideas, and feelings. -She guides open and effective communication within the family.

☐ A Boundary Setter	☐ A
-She establishes and maintains healthy boundaries within the family. -She balances each family member's individual needs with the well-being of all.	_____ -She... -She... (Write in a personalized role)

_____ + _____ = SO many roles!!

In your 50s, family roles can rival any Shakespearean play in complexity and comedy. If you're simultaneously parenting teenagers, or adult children, grandparenting, and perhaps caring for aging parents all at once, then you are in the midst of a life stage that mixes drama with unpredictability. This is the real world of *So These Are My 50s...Really!?!*

Imagine being told in your 30s that you'd become the linchpin in a multigenerational comedy of errors. Many of us find ourselves juggling responsibilities with the dexterity—and the occasional clumsiness of a circus performer who has forgotten her glasses at home, but, they are actually on her head. This life stage revolves around caring for those who once cared for us, raising children who think they've had enough raising, and spoiling grandchildren in ways our budget-conscious parents could never have imagined.

Grandparenting allows us to redo moments when discipline takes precedence over dessert. Now, we often toss discipline aside, making dessert the first course; anytime, every time. The joy of unhinged spoiling brings back the unique joy that only a grandparent understands, like, handing them back just as the sugar rush hits. This is called strategic spoiling, in grandparent language. It's a grandparent's prerogative. Don't even consider getting involved in homework with the grandchildren, as that is another minefield best avoided. Rather choose activities that are enrichment-based instead.

While reveling in the role of being a cool grandparent, you might find yourself caught between your children and your parents, spread paper-thin between both sets of responsibilities. Sometimes the stress of navigating this can feel like driving without a steering wheel while trying to explain to your aging dad that Alexa is not a new girlfriend, or to your mom that a smartphone will make her life easier, or texting your adult child for the umpteenth time about their car insurance.

Let's not overlook the comedy/tragedy of rearing adult children. These young adults still need us, but on their terms and timelines. They seek advice only after they've ignored it and learned things the hard way. Some adult children seek financial support with the casual nonchalance of someone borrowing a pen which adds even more pressure. The dynamic is a delicate dance of push and pull, where every misstep is a hidden lesson.

Caring for aging parents while figuring out your own later-life plan adds another layer of heartfelt humor to the mix. One day you are discussing retirement villages with Dad, and the next, you're buying anti-wrinkle cream together. These moments, though fraught with challenges, remind us of the importance, enduring strength, and elasticity of family bonds.

Maintaining a chuckle through it all requires an Olympic level of emotional gymnastics. It's about finding humor in the mishaps, forgetting names that turn into "Hey there... you," and the frequent travel miles you accumulate between your kids' and parents' homes.

Our 50s are not just a time of life; they're a state of mind. Here, we learn to laugh at our new roles, cry a little when no one's watching, cherish the moments of joyous spoiling, and the ever-complex family dynamics. It's an exploration of how to keep smiling through the chaos and perhaps even teach our children and grandchildren how to juggle their pending 50s with a bit of humor too.

Let's Learn About It

Acknowledging the significance of family relationships and caregiving responsibilities is integral to cultivating a sense of gratitude and mindfulness. Take time daily to reflect on the love and support received from family members and the privilege of being able to care for them in return. Expressing gratitude and appreciation through words and actions conveys their importance.

Educate yourself about the importance of family relationships and caregiving responsibilities by seeking out resources, such as books, articles, and workshops that explore these topics in-depth and offer you some support. Understanding the psychological, emotional, and physical benefits of strong family bonds and caregiving can deepen appreciation for these roles and motivate prioritization in life.

Engage in open and honest conversations with family members about the significance of relationships and the responsibilities they entail. Share thoughts and feelings openly, listening to each other's perspectives to strengthen connections and support one another through life's challenges. This is not an easy task for some to achieve as not everyone is willing to communicate openly about their feelings, particularly the older generation but start somewhere and gently persevere, it will be worth it.

When discussing evolving family dynamics, including parenting, grandparenting, and caring for aging parents, it's important to create a safe and supportive environment for open dialogue. Initiate conversations about experiences, challenges, and aspirations in their respective roles, reflecting on personal growth and evolution over time.

Explore the unique opportunities for growth and fulfillment that come with each role, offering support, encouragement, and practical advice to navigate challenges with grace and resilience.

To highlight the role of humor in strengthening family bonds and coping with the ups and downs of caregiving and family dynamics, incorporate laughter and lightheartedness into daily interactions. Share funny stories, jokes, and anecdotes to bring joy and levity to conversations and activities. Encourage a culture of humor and playfulness within the family by creating opportunities for laughter and silliness. Plan fun outings, game nights, and movie marathons that allow relaxation and enjoyment of each other's company without the pressures of daily life. Acknowledging the significance of family relationships and caregiving responsibilities, while discussing evolving family dynamics and strengthening family bonds, creates deeper connections, resilience, and joy within the family unit.

Using humor as a coping mechanism to help see the way through the challenges and stressors of caregiving and family dynamics, is hugely beneficial. Finding the lighter side of difficult situations, laughing at mistakes, and embracing the imperfections and absurdities of life with a sense of humor and perspective will go a long way, and prevent any blow-ups!

What They Didn't Tell Us

Being a caregiver simultaneously for multiple generations can present a whole bunch of unique challenges that sometimes can catch us off guard. Finding the right balance can often feel like a struggle, and much of it depends on your circumstances and where you stand concerning your children, grandchildren, and parents. Each situation is unique but one common thread is the need to manage both time and energy effectively to meet everyone's needs, including your own.

Consider a scenario where you are cooking dinner for your family, and suddenly receive a frantic phone call from your elderly parent who needs immediate assistance. It may or may not be an emergency so this could go either way! Meanwhile, your teenager needs help with his homework, and your grandchild you're babysitting for your adult child is crying for attention. The overwhelming feeling and sheer magnitude of responsibility can sometimes be too much for one person to handle. Handling this whirlwind scene of responsibilities demands a superhero-level multitasking ability, and most importantly, a good support structure.

Supporting adult children while caring for aging parents adds another layer of complexity to the caregiving dynamic. This phenomenon is known as "Boomerang Children" (Hayes, 2022). This is when adult children move back home with their parents. The COVID-19 pandemic brought this home, yes, pun intended. Young adults returning to their parent's homes after college or during periods of financial hardship are becoming more and more common. This in itself presents both challenges and opportunities for parents and adult children. This can mean all sorts of things from the benefits of gaining some extra time with them, and perhaps the grandchildren if they are on scene! But, grappling with questions about boundaries, independence, and financial support are a bit harder to deal with. Supporting adult children often requires striking a delicate balance between offering guidance and acceptance. Despite the challenges, the rewards of multigenerational caregiving are plentiful. Grandchildren are undoubtedly one of the most gratifying aspects of multigenerational caregiving. The bond between grandparents and grandchildren is a special one, filled with love, laughter, amazement, and of course endless opportunities for spoiling. It is almost like a "do-over" without the sleepless nights! Witnessing the world through a child's eyes for the second time round is immeasurable in delight and something to cherish forever. As much as we may have been told, read, or imagined, the reality of this phase of life cannot be adequately expressed in words. It must be lived to be truly understood.

Maintaining the important balance of harmony in extended family relationships is paramount, especially when conflicting personalities and competing priorities come into play. Whether it's managing family gatherings, resolving conflicts, or figuring out the intricacies of extended family dynamics, it requires patience, diplomacy, and yes, a healthy dose of good humor. Each role in the caregiving journey brings its own set of experiences and lessons. The key is to embrace both the highs and the lows, creating cherished memories with our loved ones along the way, while keeping in mind that not every family gets to experience this privilege.

Let's Laugh About It

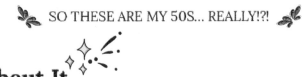

Onto the brighter side of family roles and the challenges of caregiving. An earlier chapter discussed the benefits of embracing technology in your life, but it also brought up the importance of learning patience. When it comes to your parents, patience is REQUIRED when helping them deal with all the new techno fandango...

My father decided to take on the children in a game of the latest videogame sensation which has left us with some good, funny memories. Armed with determination and a shaky grasp of modern technology, he faced the battle against his tech-savvy eldest grandson. Well, what could go wrong, you ask? My intrepid dad picks up the controller with the confidence of a seasoned pro, eager to bond with his grandchild over their shared love of games. It became a wild ride filled with desperate button smashing, joystick flailing, and more than a few choice words, along with a couple of hilarious gameplay mishaps. My dad found himself struggling to navigate the virtual world, stumbling over obstacles, and inadvertently pressing every button except the vital one! Meanwhile, my son watched on, with one eye on the game of course, alternating between amusement and disbelief at the sight of his grandfather attempting to conquer the digital realm. With every passing moment, the situation grew increasingly absurd with my dad's valiant efforts only resulting in a series of comical setbacks that would make even the most serious gamer crack a smile. It was a spectacle of epic proportions, one that left everyone in fits of laughter. You know, that acronym, ROFL—yes, that was us rolling on the floor with laughter!

That was a fun time that everyone in the family who was there still talks about today when the game eventually wound down. This was not because the grand finale had been reached, but because Dad, ever the sportsman, declared a strategic retreat, laughing heartily at his bewildering performance. It was clear that while he might not be the next gaming champion, he had unquestionably won something far more precious. A time that brought the generations closer together. So, let's laugh about our family moments because sometimes, through these imperfect, silly times we truly understand the love and resilience that define a family. With each new challenge and every blooper we encounter, we are reminded that being there for each other, in laughter and patience, is what truly matters.

How to Engage and Embrace the Changes

Not all families get along and some may require clearer boundaries than others.

In the whirlwind of multitasking and juggling multiple caregiving responsibilities, setting these boundaries and managing family expectations becomes paramount. Here are some practical tips for dealing with these challenges and the crucial role of self-care for caregivers.

Setting boundaries and managing family expectations

- Communicate openly and clearly with your family members, as it is essential for any hope of success. Schedule regular family meetings and jot down everyone's thoughts, to discuss caregiving responsibilities, address concerns, and set expectations. Encourage everyone to share their thoughts and feelings openly. A supportive and understanding environment is what is key, allowing everyone to feel that they have been heard.

- Define your priorities and identify your core priorities, allocating time and energy appropriately. Determine which tasks are non-negotiable, and where you can delegate or seek assistance. Setting these boundaries clearly around your time and resources helps to prevent burnout and ensures that the focus remains on what truly matters.

- Learn to say no. This has been mentioned previously but deserves another mention, particularly with family dynamics. It is perfectly okay to decline additional responsibilities or commitments that may overwhelm you. Practice assertiveness and assert your needs respectfully but firmly. Saying no doesn't make you selfish; it's an act of self-preservation and self-care.

- Don't hesitate to delegate tasks and enlist the help of other family members, friends, or professional caregivers. These tasks can be divided up based on each person's strengths and availability. Sharing the caregiving load creates a sense of collaboration and prevents one person from shouldering the burden unsupported.

- Prioritize activities and self-care routines that replenish your physical and emotional well-being. Regular breaks, participation in activities, and hobbies that nurture your self-worth are so important. This could be riding your bike, playing cards, meditation, or yoga. It doesn't matter what it is; what matters is that whatever you do allows you to recharge and be more present for your loved ones.

Success stories of finding balance in family roles

Julie's Story: Julie, a busy mother of three, felt overwhelmed by the demands of caregiving for her aging parents while raising her young children. By openly discussing her challenges with her spouse and siblings, she was able to delegate specific tasks and establish a solid support network. She also prioritized self-care by scheduling regular exercise sessions and participating in a monthly book club. Through effective communication and self-care practices, Julie found balance in her family roles and regained a sense of control over her life.

Lila's Journey: Lila, a full-time caregiver for her disabled son, struggled to find time for herself amidst her demanding caregiving responsibilities. With the encouragement of her support group, she began prioritizing self-care activities such as journaling, gardening, and attending art therapy sessions. She also learned to set boundaries with well-meaning family members and friends who often imposed additional demands on her time. By honoring her needs and prioritizing self-care, Lila experienced a renewed sense of purpose and resilience in her caregiving journey.

Ruth's Reflections: Ruth, a career-driven professional, faced challenges in balancing her demanding job with her role as a caregiver for her aging parents. Through trial and error, she discovered the importance of time management and prioritization. She created a daily schedule that allowed her to allocate dedicated time for work, caregiving, and personal pursuits. Ruth also sought support from her employer, negotiating flexible work arrangements and access to employee assistance programs. By implementing practical strategies and seeking support, Ruth successfully navigated the complexities of caregiving while maintaining her career aspirations.

June's Journey: June, a retired teacher, found herself caring for her grandchildren while their parents worked long hours. Initially overwhelmed by the responsibility, June learned to establish boundaries and communicate her needs effectively. She enlisted the help of other grandparents in the community, forming a support network for childcare and emotional support. June also prioritized self-care by attending weekly yoga classes and volunteering at a local charity. Through collaboration and self-care practices, June found fulfillment in her role as a caregiver and maintained a healthy balance in her life.

Accepting and engaging with the changes that come with caregiving involves setting these boundaries, managing family expectations, and prioritizing self-care. By communicating openly, defining priorities, and learning to say no, caregivers can clarify their responsibilities more effectively. These success stories of women who have found balance in their family roles serve as inspiration and encouragement for others facing similar challenges. Through proactive measures and a commitment to self-care, caregivers can thrive in their caregiving journey while maintaining their well-being.

Chapter 8- My Family Roles

ToDo 1 - Acrostic Poem

Think about and decide on one word that defines a role you are currently fulfilling in your family. See the word cloud to help you choose, if you'd like. Use your selected word to write an Acrostic poem all about you! Acrostic poems simply use the first letter of a vertically written word to guide the text of the poem (see example).

Mirthful laughter fills the air, a precious sound so sweet,

Overflowing hearts with love, in motherhood's complete.

Tender touches, gentle hugs, in every moment found,

Healing wounds and drying tears, with care that knows no bound.

Eternal bonds of love and trust, in every smile we see,

Radiant beacon of light, a mother's legacy.

Engage, Embrace, Empower: YOU!

ToDo1 - write your poem below...

cleaner librarian technician spiritual

repairer **organizer leader** **historian** **advocate**

bookkeeper guardian

problem-solver **model** **cheerleader** nurturer translator

personal grandmother educator **travel**

companion **teacher** **mentor** family inspiration

arbitrator **supporter** **role** **comforter** breadwinner

motivator mother empowerer

listener aunt **manager** advisor agent

confidante daughter sister chef solver

strategist crisis **mediator** **disciplinarian**

problem homemaker **coach** **innovator** maker volunteer guide

fashion caretaker **planner** provider gardener

time **financial** nurse caregiver

negotiator protector

networker chauffeur vote scheduler event friend counselor storyteller

emotional seamstress decision homesteader cook

assistant encourager budgeter

connector

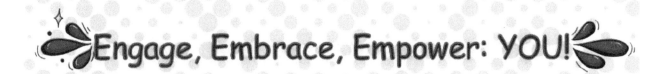

Engage, Embrace, Empower: YOU!

ToDo 2- Self-Care Collage

Gather a bunch of magazines, scissors, glue, and a poster board. Create a collage representing your ideal self-care practices, incorporating activities and hobbies that replenish/recharge your physical and emotional well-being. Display this in your bathroom or bedroom.

ToDo 3- Boundaries Journal

Reflect on a time when you struggled to maintain a family boundary, but you were resilient and persevered. Describe the challenges you faced and how you overcame them. Or, consider how the success stories shared in the chapter resonate with your own experiences and inspire you to prioritize self-care in your caregiving journey.

_____

_____

_____

_____

_____

_____

_____

_____

_____

_____

_____

_____

_____

_____

Engage, Embrace, Empower: YOU!

Falling in Love With Your Family Roles

Have you ever thought of your role as a parent, grandparent, or caregiver as something to fall in love with? It might sound a little unconventional but it can become a source of fulfillment rather than a burden. In this last chapter, we'll celebrate the stories of remarkable women who have discovered profound joy in their various roles. Through their experiences, we'll uncover the power of laughter and shared traditions in forging deep connections with our loved ones.

Meet Maria, a devoted daughter who suddenly found herself thrust into the role of caregiver for her aging parents. Initially overwhelmed by the responsibility, she soon discovered the advantages of spending all this extra time with her parents and reconnecting through shared experiences. Balancing work, personal needs, and their care became quite a juggling act. But, it created a deeper connection, particularly during those tender moments of companionship. This newfound bond that had been formed with her parents somehow made the hardships less challenging, and she found fulfillment in being able to be there for her parents when they needed her most, despite the difficulties.

Then there's Teresa, a single mother in her 50s, who juggled the ever-changing needs of her teenage children alongside caring for her disabled brother. The days were a constant whirlwind of balancing school activities, doctor's appointments, and her work deadlines. Gone were the days of chilling on the couch, or cuddling up with her children reading them bedtime stories. It became a little nostalgic and sad, and her energy levels weren't what they used to be, but Teresa had unwavering love and determination. She shifted her focus and embraced a new parenting style, offering guidance instead of micromanagement. She discovered hidden reserves of strength, fueled by her unwavering love for her family. Teresa thrived in the chaos, proving that love and determination can conquer even the most unique challenges of being a single mom and caregiver in your 50s.

Anne, a grandmother, discovered a newfound sense of purpose in caring for her grandchildren. She missed the nurturing aspect of motherhood and craved a fresh challenge, and also, she had become a little bored with the hobbies that filled her days. She was more than ready for some responsibility to step in and help her children who were busy setting up a new business. This situation of providing care for her grandchildren was not only helpful to her children, but it also nurtured a deeper love and a renewed connection with both them, and her grandchildren. Through storytelling, baking sessions, and exciting outdoor explorations, they created cherished memories that will last a lifetime. The joy and fulfillment Anne experienced were beyond measure, reaffirming the enduring importance of family bonds in her life.

Laughter has a remarkable ability to unite us, to dissolve barriers, and to strengthen the bonds of family. Shared jokes, playful banter, and moments of pure joy bring us closer and remind us of the inherent joy in family life.

Let's welcome the profound truth with open arms that our family roles are not burdens, but invitations. Invitations to connect, to nurture, to create a legacy of love that transcends generations. Shared traditions, like threads woven into a tapestry, are the tangible expressions of this love. Whether it's the laughter echoing from a simple Sunday brunch tradition or the quiet comfort of a familiar holiday ritual, these traditions anchor us in a shared history and create a sense of belonging.

Falling in love with your family role isn't about achieving perfection; it's about embracing these imperfections, the mishaps that become cherished stories to be repeated over and over again. It's about finding joy in the every day, in the quiet moment of connection that blossoms amid the chaos. It's about recognizing the profound gift of family, a messy, beautiful tapestry woven with love, laughter, and shared experiences. The moments of tenderness that linger in your heart.

So, step into your role whatever it may be, with open arms, embracing the challenges and savoring the victories. You might just discover that falling in love with your family role is the greatest adventure of all.

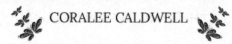

Fall In Love with: YOURSELF!

Chapter 8- My Family Roles

ToDo 1- Family Meal Time

Host a family meal with the intent to have a time to share anecdotes, family history, or tales to entertain and bond with your family. This is a great way to pass down traditions, and memories across generations. What you share is what you value!

ToDo 2- Funny Family Moments

Create a special moments book that all family members have access to. Any lined journal will do, but make sure your family name, or monogram is written in on the front; use fancy markers or a cutting machine to add this! Inside, note each date and write down funny moments, jokes, or any funny memories you have shared. Remember all those things your kids said that made you crack up? How about when Grandpa was trying to get the Christmas tree to stand straight and split his pants while everyone was watching? Go back through the years, but more importantly, continue to fill in this book as your family grows and changes. Start a new tradition where you read a few out loud every Thanksgiving or New Year's Eve.

Fall In Love with: YOURSELF!

ToDo 3- Family Roles & Contributions Reflection

Reflect on one distinct, positive, memorable occasion in your life with your family. Describe the roles and contributions each family member played.

If this same occasion were to happen today, how might these roles have evolved, and what impact would these changes have on your family dynamics today?

_____

_____

_____

_____

_____

_____

_____

_____

_____

_____

_____

_____

_____

_____

_____

_____

_____

_____

Conclusion

As we conclude our exploration of "So *These Are My 50s... Really!?!*" it's essential to take a moment to reflect on the journey we've shared.

Choosing to divide each chapter into four sections provides a flexible roadmap for easy referencing and reviewing of the book's content, allowing you to extract inspiration or motivation as needed.

- Let's Learn About It: This section delivers insightful information, facts, or lessons for you to absorb and learn from, serving as a foundation for personal growth and development. When reflecting on what has been read, you can swiftly refer back to specific information or insights on particular topics.

- Let's Laugh About It: Laughter, a powerful tool for stress relief and mood enhancement, fills this section with humor, anecdotes, or light-hearted stories. When feeling low or in need of a lift, you can easily turn to this section for moments of joy and upliftment.

- How to Engage and Embrace the Changes: Encouraging active participation, this section offers activities, exercises, or reflections designed to promote self-discovery and personal engagement. Revisiting this section in the future allows for engagement in exercises that resonate with you at different stages of your journey.

• Fall In Love: Highlighting beauty, inspiration, and positivity, this section showcases moments of wonder and appreciation for life's intricacies. Immersing ourselves in this section enables us to reignite passion, cultivate gratitude, and rediscover what we love about ourselves and the world around us.

Completing all activities in each section is encouraged, even if they need modification to suit your individual needs or preferences. Each activity provides unique benefits and insights, contributing to a holistic experience of growth and enrichment. Remember, the journey of self-discovery is ongoing, with each step bringing you closer to your fullest potential.

Reflect on the Journey

From the highs to the lows, from body changes to energy loss, the laughter to the tears, each chapter has been a testament to the complexity and beauty of this remarkable decade. We've delved into the depths of our bodies, hearts, minds, and relationships, uncovering insights and wisdom along the way. Through laughter and engagement, we've embraced the challenges and triumphs of our 50s, knowing that we are not alone in our experiences.

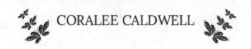

Embrace Each Day

As we move forward, let us embrace each day with gratitude and purpose. Our 50s are a time of renewal and growth, a chance to rediscover ourselves and our passions. Whether it's nurturing our bodies, cultivating our relationships, pursuing our dreams, learning a new skill, or pursuing a long-desired hobby, let us seize each moment with intention and enthusiasm. Let us celebrate the gift of life and the opportunity to make a difference in the world around us, no matter how big or small.

Embrace the Future

As we look to the future, let us embrace the possibilities that lie ahead and not get stuck in the past. Think of all the possibilities from travel, and career changes, to pursuing entrepreneurial dreams. Our 50s are not the end of our journey but the beginning of a new chapter filled with endless opportunities. Let us approach the future with optimism and courage, knowing that we have the strength and resilience to overcome any obstacle. Let us dare to dream big and pursue our goals with determination and perseverance.

The Power of Humor

Throughout our journey, we've discovered the transformative power of humor. Laughter has been our constant companion, helping us navigate the ups and downs of life with grace and resilience. Let us never underestimate the power of laughter to heal, uplift, and unite us. Let us continue to find joy in the everyday moments and embrace the lighter side of life. As I envisioned this book, I realized laughter isn't just a pleasant side effect of navigating our 50s—it's a powerful tool. Laughter became a thread woven through

each chapter, a reminder that joy and humor can be our companions even through all life's complexities.

Stay Connected

As we move forward, let us stay connected to ourselves and each other. Our 50s are a time to cherish our relationships and nurture the bonds that sustain us. Consistently reach out to loved ones, offering support, encouragement, and companionship. Let us celebrate our connections' richness and the joy of shared experiences.

Set New Goals

As we conclude our journey, let us set new goals and aspirations for the future. Our 50s are a time of possibility and potential, a chance to pursue our passions and fulfill our dreams. Let us challenge ourselves to step outside our comfort zones, embrace new opportunities, and strive for excellence in all that we do. Let us never stop growing, learning, and evolving as individuals.

Final Thoughts

In closing, "*So These Are My 50s... Really!?!*" has been more than just a book—it's been a personal journey for me, a roadmap, a companion, and a source of inspiration for navigating the complexities of our 50s. As we continue to the next chapter of our lives, let us carry the lessons learned and the memories shared as we continue to learn, laugh, engage, and fall in love with each moment, knowing that ALL women have been, will be, or are experiencing the same things.

Together, let us embrace the adventure of our 50s with courage, grace, and a sense of humor. Here's to the journey ahead and to the women we are becoming. Ultimately, choosing to gift this book to a friend is more than just sharing stories, it represents an act of love, conveying, "I cherish our bond and aspire to enhance your life with depth." Exploring these pages with a book club, where each sentence ignites vibrant conversations and collective revelations embodies the epitome of the support we strive to cultivate; uniting, exchanging narratives, and discovering comfort, love, and joy in each other's presence.

Cheers!

About the Author

Coralee Caldwell is a clever and passionate wordplay addict with advanced degrees in both English and Sociology. Since retiring from formal teaching, she now brings a wealth of life experience and academic acumen to both adult literature and children's books. Her stories weave tales that blend humor, insight, and a keen understanding of the twists and turns in life's journeys. Her writing shares her sharp wit and the ability to navigate the complexities of life with a lighthearted touch. This unique style combines humor with observations, resulting in narratives that are not only amusing but also strikingly on point. Readers will travel journeys that make them laugh out loud while recognizing themselves in shared experiences.

Beyond her academic and literary achievements, Ms. Caldwell's multiracial heritage adds dimension to her personal stories, offering readers a nuanced perspective on identity and diversity. Widowed but undeterred, she tries to always find joy in the simple pleasures of life, particularly in the making and eating of pasta, and in spoiling her beloved Yorkshire Terriers.

Ms. Caldwell's writing isn't mere entertainment; it serves as a mirror reflecting the human experience in all its eclectic, humorous, and poignant glory. Her work is a celebration of life's quirks- a reminder to find laughter everyday- through her insightful and delightful prose.

References

Ackerman, C. E. (2017, February 28). What is gratitude and why is it so important? Positive Psychology. https://positivepsychology.com/gratitude-appreciation/

Alcon, A. (1999). *Financial planning and the mature woman.* FPA. https://www.financialplanningassociation.org/article/journal/FEB99-financial-planning-and-mature-woman

Badshah, N. (2023, April 19). Scientists may have discovered why hair turns grey. *The Guardian.* https://www.theguardian.com/science/2023/apr/19/scientists-may-have-discovered-why-hair-turns-grey

Ballard Brown, T. (2021, September 16). *Dating over 50: It's OK to be nervous, but don't let that stop you.* NPR. https://www.npr.org/2021/09/13/1036793960/dating-over-50-guide-advice-tips

Bloomenthal, A. (2023). *How to save for retirement in your 50's.* Forbes. https://www.forbes.com/advisor/retirement/save-for-retirement-in-your-50s/

Boehm, J. K., & Kubzansky, L. D. (2012). The heart's content: The association between positive psychological well-being and cardiovascular health. *Psychological Bulletin, 138*(4), 655–691.

Booth, F. W., Roberts, C. K., & Laye, M. J. (2012). Lack of exercise is a major cause of chronic diseases. *Comprehensive Physiology*, 2(2). https://doi.org/10.1002/cphy.c110025

Britannica. (2019a). GIF | digital file format. In *Encyclopædia Britannica*. https://www.britannica.com/technology/GIF

Britannica. (2019b). GIF | digital file format. In *Encyclopædia Britannica*. https://www.britannica.com/technology/GIF

Carstensen, L., Isaacowitz, D., & Charles, S. (2024). Taking time seriously: A theory of socioemotional selectivity. *American Psychologist*, 54(3), 165–181. https://doi.org/10.1037/0003-066X.54.3.165

Carter, C. (2020, August 12). *What should your diet be like at 50+?* AARP. https://www.aarp.org/health/healthy-living/info-2020/nutrition-after-age-50.html

Chatzky, J. (2019). *Women with money: The judgment-free guide to creating the joyful, less stressed, purposeful (and, yes, rich) life you deserve*. Grand Central Publishing.

Davis, J. L. (2024). *Natural beauty tips for women over 50*. WebMD. https://www.webmd.com/beauty/women-over-50-natural-beauty-tips

Fagan, C. & Ver Hage, L. (2018). *The Financial Diet: A total beginner's guide to getting good with money*. Holt Paperbacks.

Fischer, D. B. (2024). *Are neck wrinkles telling your age?* Beverly Fischer Blog. https://www.beverlyfischer.net/blog/neck-telling-your-age

Forbes Profile. (2024). *Oprah Winfrey*. Forbes. https://www.forbes.com/profile/oprah-winfrey/?sh=5521fb355745

Garfield, J. A. (n.d.). *James A. Garfield quotes*. A-Z Quotes. https://www.azquotes.com/quote/106564

Gelhoren, D. G. T., Gray, D., Teti, J., & Gelhoren, G. (2024, March 11). *49 times celeb women rocked their gorgeous gray hair on the red carpet*. SheKnows. https://www.sheknows.com/entertainment/slideshow/2469158/celebrity-women-gray-hair-red-carpet-photos/1/

Harvard Health. (2019, March 21). *Benefits of mindfulness*. HelpGuide.org. https://www.helpguide.org/harvard/benefits-of-mindfulness.htm

Hattersley, C. (2022, April 21). *Ultimate guide to spring fashion trends for women over 50*. Cindy Hattersley Design. https://cindyhattersleydesign.com/spring-trends-women-over-50/

Hayes, A. (2022). *Boomerang children*. Investopedia. https://www.investopedia.com/terms/b/boomerangs.asp

Hofmann, S. G., & Gómez, A. F. (2019). Mindfulness-based interventions for anxiety and depression. *Psychiatric Clinics of North America, 40*(4), 739–749. https://doi.org/10.1016/j.psc.2017.08.008

IronMan. (2022, May 8). *How to stay fit in your 50s and beyond*. Ironman Magazine. https://www.ironmanmagazine.com/how-to-stay-fit-in-your-50s-and-beyond/

Leaf, C. (2023). *Why do we need to fall in love with our emotions?* LinkedIn. https://www.linkedin.com/pulse/why-we-need-fall-love-our-emotions-dr-caroline-leaf/

Mcleod, S. (2024, January 25). *Erik Erikson's stages of psychosocial development*. Simply Psychology.

Mind Tools. (2023). SMART goals. Mind Tools. https://www.mindtools.com/a4wo118/smart-goals

Mind Tools Content Team. (2022). What is time management? Mind Tools. https://www.mindtools.com/arb6j5a/what-is-time-management

NHS. (2022). Overview - cognitive behavioral therapy (CBT). NHS UK. https://www.nhs.uk/mental-health/talking-therapies-medicine-treatments/talking-therapies-and-counselling/cognitive-behavioural-therapy-cbt/overview/

Perry, E. (2023). How to get motivated: 19 ways to give yourself a boost. Betterup. https://www.betterup.com/blog/how-to-get-motivated

Ritchie, H., & Roser, M. (2019, September 20). Age structure. Our World in Data. https://ourworldindata.org/age-structure

Rogers, K. (2020, November 5). The top 5 ways I learned to love my body at age 50. Nutritious Life. https://nutritiouslife.com/nurture-yourself/5-ways-i-learned-to-love-my-body-at-age-50/

Sapolin, D. (2013, February 18). 9 best things about being over 50. Next Avenue. https://www.nextavenue.org/9-best-things-about-being-over-50/

Schmerling, R. (2017, September 18). Why does hair turn gray? Harvard Health Blog. https://www.health.harvard.edu/blog/hair-turn-gray-2017091812226

Segal, J., Smith, M., Robinson, L., & Segal, R. (2023, April 5). Stress symptoms, signs, and causes: Improving your ability to handle stress. Helpguide.org. https://www.helpguide.org/articles/stress/stress-symptoms-signs-and-causes.htm

Southwick, S. M., Bonanno, G. A., Masten, A. S., Panter-Brick, C., & Yehuda, R. (2014). Resilience definitions, theory, and challenges: Interdisciplinary perspectives. *European Journal of Psychotraumatology*, 5(1), 25338. https://doi.org/10.3402/ejpt.v5.25338

Swiner, C. (2021, June 29). *What to expect in your 50s*. WebMD. https://www.webmd.com/healthy-aging/ss/slideshow-what-to-expect-in-your-50s

Umberson, D., Crosnoe, R., & Reczek, C. (2010). Social relationships and health behavior across the life course. *Annual Review of Sociology*, 36(1), 139–157. https://doi.org/10.1146/annurev-soc-070308-120011

United States Attorney's Office. (2015, April 8). *Protecting yourself while using the internet*. Justice.gov. https://www.justice.gov/usao-ndga/protecting-yourself-while-using-internet

WebMD. (2023). *Which type of estrogen hormone therapy is right for you?* WebMD. https://www.webmd.com/menopause/which-type-of-estrogen-hormone-therapy-is-right-for-you

Wikipedia Editors. (2019, March 24). *Girls just want to have fun*. Wikipedia; Wikimedia Foundation. https://en.wikipedia.org/wiki/Girls_Just_Want_to_Have_Fun

Wikipedia Editors. (2020, August 30). *Iris Apfel*. Wikipedia. https://en.wikipedia.org/wiki/Iris_Apfel

Wikipedia Editors. (2019, December 16). *Julia Child*. Wikipedia; Wikimedia Foundation. https://en.wikipedia.org/wiki/Julia_Child

Wikipedia Editors. (2019, January 17). *Michelle Obama*. Wikipedia; Wikimedia Foundation. https://en.wikipedia.org/wiki/Michelle_Obama

Wooll, M. (2022). *How to start over in life at 50: It's never too late*. Betterup. https://www.betterup.com/blog/how-to-start-over-in-life-at-50

Wrightman, C., & Sissons, B. (2022, February 15). *Dermatologist-recommended skin care: Tips and routine*. Medical News Today. https://www.medicalnewstoday.com/articles/dermatologist-recommended-skin-care

QR Links Coming Soon

Links Coming Soon

Made in the USA
Monee, IL
06 October 2024

67324075R00136